PRAISE FOR *CONNECTED*

"An unbeatable roadmap for improving the
most important relationships in your life."
MEL ROBBINS, *New York Times* bestselling author
and host of *The Mel Robbins Podcast*

"*Connected* provides a new fast track to unlimited success.
With an engaging blend of art and science,
Patricia Bathory shows how to build relationships
that elevate every aspect of our lives."
JOSH LINKNER, five-time tech entrepreneur,
New York Times bestselling author, and venture capitalist

"*Connected* offers convincing evidence that pursuing
happiness isn't as effective or inspiring as pursuing
a meaningful purpose that evokes happiness. Patricia Bathory
offers a fresh and practical approach to success that's
rooted in her entrepreneurial background and enriched
with her experience as a psychotherapist."
AMMAR CHARANI, founder of
YPO Changemakers Club and author of
Purposehood: Transform Your Life, Transform the World

"No matter what we want to achieve, we need a village. In *Connected*, Patricia Bathory shows how to develop strong, authentic relationships that accelerate success and enhance our ability to make a positive difference in the world."
BRAD ARONSON, author of the national bestseller
HumanKind: Changing the World One Small Act at a Time

"One of the most effective ways to reduce conflict is to become adept at relationship skills. The inspiring stories and scientific research in *Connected* illustrate that our relationships have the most influence on whether we'll achieve our personal and professional goals. The guidance Patricia Bathory provides will equip you with the knowledge, insights, and tools to build a village that will help you become the person you aspire to be."
JUDY BACHMANN, former family lawyer, mediator, arbitrator, and parenting coordinator

"I've always believed that happiness relies on having good relationships and strong connections. This book presents the research that explains why, and shows you how to make sure your relationships work for you instead of against you."
RODRIGO XAVIER, former CEO of Bank of America Merrill Lynch (Brazil), current senior partner of YvY Capital, and board member of Globo and B3

"Many people ask me what the secret to my company's growth is. They ask how we came up with an idea, how we made a specific technological innovation, or how we raised money. But the real secret to our success is our purpose—and our people who help us achieve it. Patricia Bathory understands that creating strong relationships is essential so we can collaborate, grow, and make a positive difference in our communities and our world. *Connected* shows you how to do just that."

FABRICIO BLOISI, CEO and founder of iFood, founder of Movile, president of Fundação 1Bi

amplify
an imprint of Amplify Publishing Group

www.amplifypublishinggroup.com

Connected: Building Relationships to Achieve Success and Make a Lasting Impact

The stories in this book are true, but the author has changed many of the details to protect the identity and privacy of her clients. The dialogue the author has included is often paraphrased and sometimes embellished to include conversations from other sessions. The details have been altered to ensure that no reader can identify any of the real-life clients.

For more information, please contact:

Amplify Publishing, an imprint of Amplify Publishing Group

620 Herndon Parkway, Suite 220

Herndon, VA 20170

info@amplifypublishing.com

Library of Congress Control Number: 2023916808

CPSIA Code: PRV1223A

ISBN-13: 979-8-89138-041-7

Printed in the United States

To Bela and Sasa, loving you has been the most profound experience in my life. You are masterpieces—the best contribution and most perfect legacy I'll leave to this world.

To Lauro, I'm so fortunate to have you—the best partner for building a life full of meaning and purpose. You inspire me to do better every day.

To Dad, thank you for keeping me in your prayers.

To Mom, Roberta, and Tico, if it weren't for you, I'd be a much lesser version of me. I am grateful every day for your love and the privilege of growing up in our home with you.

CONNECTED

Building Relationships
to Achieve Success and
Make a Lasting Impact

PATRICIA BATHORY

amplify
an imprint of Amplify Publishing Group

CONTENTS

Introduction   xi

Chapter 1
To Make a Lasting Impact, Master the Art of Connecting   1

Chapter 2
Purpose Makes Life More Meaningful   19

Chapter 3
It Takes a Village to Leave a Legacy   43

Chapter 4
Rate Your Own Game   69

Chapter 5
Upgrade Your Communication Skills   91

Chapter 6
Adopt Relationship Best Practices   113

Chapter 7
Build Your Village   133

Chapter 8
Navigate Compatibility Differences   157

Chapter 9
Make a Lasting Impact   181

Relationship Action Guide
Reconnect, Remodel, and Repair   195

Endnotes   223

Acknowledgments   229

Big Brothers Big Sisters of America   233

About the Author   237

INTRODUCTION

I've loved the African proverb "It takes a village to raise a child" from the first time I heard it. But it wasn't until I had my own children that the concept really hit home. Raising Bela and Sasa was only possible because my village was there to help me: my husband Lauro, my family and friends, teachers, doctors, nannies, nutritionists, and therapists all played a role in shaping the young women my daughters are today.

Because I have such a strong, supportive village, I was able to start an import/export business and continue to run it as I raised my daughters. When I founded Paroti Comex, I'd just completed my MBA in Canada and knew very little about the laws and regulations for importing from Brazil or the FDA regulations about exporting food to the United States. But I had a friend who told me about a small customs clearance office nearby, so I showed up with a batch of Brazilian cheese breads called *pão de queijo* and asked if I could help out in exchange for learning the business. Lucia and Wellington accepted my proposal, so every Wednesday for eight months I showed up with *pão de queijo* and learned everything they could teach me.

As my knowledge and passion grew, so did my village. Eduardo, the owner of the factory that produced the juices I exported, generously taught me about the juice business, from the product technicalities to fun facts about the process. I was free to experiment with formulas, and he was willing to custom-make the products my clients wanted. We developed new flavors and a few private labels, and the business took off.

But I needed to pay for the product up front and give my clients credit for sixty days after shipment, so my husband stepped up and lent me quite a bit of money for those initial containers. The company also needed a meeting room, an accountant and a lawyer, so my father-in-law included me in his business's company bundle package and made all those things available to me. I got *a lot* of help from my village.

Fifteen years later, when the work I did with my therapist inspired me to become one myself, my daughters were nine and thirteen. They were already independent and self-sufficient, but I wouldn't have been comfortable with going back to school at that time if my village didn't have my back. Our nanny, Iva, who we affectionately called "The Boss," ran our house like a tight ship. Aunt Marilu was the emergency contact for the girls when we were out of town. When Sasa needed a place to go after school, my sister-in-law Lara welcomed her, and Bela's friends' parents gave her rides to parties. I still marvel at how everyone stepped up to help.

These personal experiences, together with decades of studying psychology, philosophy, and theology, have shown me that *all* significant accomplishments take a village, whether we're raising healthy children, running a successful business or pursuing our life purpose. Behind every success story, there's a cast of characters who helped make it happen. Nobody who's made a lasting impact has done it alone. And since we need good interpersonal skills to build and grow a village, there is a direct correlation between them and our success.

As the research and stories in this book illustrate, healthy connections are at the root of every successful venture and undertaking. So the objective of the book is to help you to identify your purpose and build relationships that can help you to achieve whatever is most meaningful to you. (If you haven't identified what you'd love to accomplish, no problem. Chapter Two is all about that.)

When I say that improving your ability to relate to and connect with others is the best investment you can make, I'm not exaggerating. Time and again, clients' lives transform before my eyes—all because they do the work to become better at making strong connections. Doing the work can include anything from increasing self awareness to healing childhood wounds to upgrading your communication skills. Self-improvement and strengthening the relationship you have with yourself will also help you improve your relationship with others. And everything you do to improve your rapport with others increases your chances of achieving success and making a lasting impact.

RELATIONSHIP SKILLS GIVE YOU AN EDGE

Helping my clients to become who they aspire to be and improve their relationships are the most rewarding things I do, because that improves their health, enhances their happiness and positions them for greater success—whatever that means to them. When your connections are strong and supportive, you can invest your energy in actions that are meaningful and purposeful. When they're not, a lot of time and energy can be drained by unnecessary conflict and drama. My clients' biggest struggles are often eliminated by improving their relationship skills, and they're usually surprised by how much time and effort that saves. They'll be the first ones to tell you that the work wasn't easy, but they'll also say it was well worth it.

I'm a psychotherapist, but that doesn't mean relationships are easy for me. I've had to work hard on myself to build strong connections, so I'm writing from a place of empathy as well as a place of certainty. Yes, it can be hard to get along with some people, but it's a skill you *can* learn and continue to improve throughout your life. It's like swimming—you can practice just enough to keep your head above water or enough to become smooth and proficient. If your interpersonal skills are only strong enough to keep you from drowning, you're missing out on so much that life has to offer. So I hope the research and stories I've included will assure you that:

- Good relationships are vital for a successful life— however you define success.
- You can become very good at building and developing strong connections.
- If you have a purpose you want to achieve or a lasting impact you want to make, you're more likely to succeed if you have a village behind you.

I also hope you do the exercises I've included because your observations and insights will guide you to define success on your terms, decide what you want to accomplish or achieve, and help you to build relationships that are aligned with whatever is most meaningful to you. To get the most out of the exercises, do them in a notebook or on your computer so you can refer back to them throughout the book and afterward.

FEED THE WHEEL OF GOOD

My life purpose is to make a positive contribution to other people's lives, whether that's by guiding them to close the gap between who they are and who they aspire to be, offering a new perspective, helping them to find hope or solve a problem, or supporting them through a major transition or crisis. I decided to write this book because relationship issues cause a great deal of suffering, lower our productivity, and undermine even the best-laid plans. A friend of mine who runs a paint production company summed it up when he said, "Having state-of-the-art machinery is useless if the guy who's operating it isn't getting along with his wife or found out his kid has been lying to him." When we're dealing with personal problems, our ability to focus and do good work declines significantly. So I wanted this book to help make people's lives easier and more successful, and I wanted it to create a ripple effect, with one strong connection leading to another. In this way, I could contribute to the wheel of good and help make the world at least a little better for some people.

And after meeting Brad Aronson, author of *HumanKind: Changing the World One Small Act at a Time*, I decided I wanted the book to feed the wheel of good in two ways: by supporting readers and by supporting kids, like Brad's book is doing. Brad donates his book's proceeds to nonprofit organizations that provide young people with mentoring and other important forms of support. When he shared that with me, I knew I wanted my book to support young people too. So I decided to give the proceeds to Big Brothers Big Sisters of America because the relationships they facilitate between children and adults have a lasting positive impact on the children's lives. (You can read more about the organization on page 233.)

Whether you share my belief that we're all connected or not, we've all seen one kind act or word lead to another. By taking the initiative to become better at building strong connections, not only do we benefit ourselves but we can also positively influence the people in our villages and communities. And with the ripple effect, we might even touch someone on the other side of the world. Ready?

CHAPTER 1

TO MAKE A LASTING IMPACT, MASTER THE ART OF CONNECTING

For the former president and CEO of Ri Happy, Brazil's largest toy sales company, good isn't good enough. From the time Ronaldo Pereira was a child, he wanted to be the best at everything. Whether it was getting the highest grades in his class, selling the most chocolate bars for the school fundraiser, or running the fifty-meter dash, he aimed for the top. "Fighting to be the best made me be among the best," he says. "That was always my goal."

Ronaldo didn't want an easy life. He wanted the best that life had to offer, including the best education. So when he learned that the Colégio Naval in Angra dos Reis was one of the best high schools in Brazil, he started devising a plan for getting accepted. First, he found out he'd have the best chance if he attended the Colégio Martins prep school in eighth grade, and he made up his mind that that's where he needed to go. The fact that the school was in the capital city—more than eighty miles (130 km) from his home—didn't discourage him.

To reach that initial goal, he used the same approaches he uses today: problem-solving and reaching out to his network. "If there's a problem, there's a solution," he says. "If we want to be successful, treating problems like opportunities isn't just a motivational saying—it's a way of life. I knew I could find a way to go to Colégio Martins. I didn't think about the obstacles. Day and night, I thought about how I could make it happen and who I knew that might be able to help me." He smiles. "That's when I remembered that my grandparents' good friends Chagas and Miriam lived in Rio, and they'd always treated me like I was one of their own grandkids."

So Ronaldo told them about his dream to attend the naval high school. "I asked if I could live with them for the school year and they said yes. They didn't even hesitate." He laughs. "Getting a yes from my mom and dad wasn't so easy, but I was relentless, so they let me go."

At that time, the naval high school was one of the most prestigious schools in Brazil and one of the hardest ones to get into, so Ronaldo's classes at the prep school ended up being more challenging than he'd expected. He was determined to excel, though, so not only did he spend a lot of time studying, but he also learned how to become *better* at studying. "I made friends with my classmates that got the best grades," he says. "Studying with them definitely made me a better student."

When he wasn't studying, one of his favorite pastimes was hearing about Chagas's experiences as an executive at Philco Hitachi. Over fiercely competitive games of *buraco*, Ronaldo learned about the challenges Chagas had faced and how he triumphed. While the cards were being shuffled, Chagas would tell stories about the people he worked with and how he became friends with so many of them. Trust and making decisions for the greater good were recurring themes of the stories, and Ronaldo took those messages to heart.

"In business relationships, nothing is more valuable than trust," he says. "Of course, experience is important, but in the end the person who gets the job or gets offered a partnership or gets a loan is the one who can be trusted. If you don't create a network of people who know you're trustworthy, your opportunities may be limited. It's not just who you know—it's also who knows *you*."

The importance of building trust was also a theme of the stories that Chagas's son Paulo told Ronaldo. Paulo owned a successful lumber business, and Ronaldo quizzed him about best business practices every chance he had.

Between his new role models, school, and living in the capital city, Ronaldo learned more in one year than he would have thought possible. "It made me work harder and reach higher than I ever had before. It also gave me a chance to see the truth in what Chagas and Paulo said about relationships. Many of my classmates' parents were successful, and they all were surrounded with people they trusted and had big networks."

When Ronaldo sat down to take the entrance exam for the naval high school at the end of the school year, he had visions of wearing a sharp white uniform and plans for some well-earned time at the beach. So when he received the letter saying he hadn't been admitted, he was devastated. "It was two strikes in one," he says, "not getting into naval school and having to move back to Barra Mansa."

While not being accepted to the naval school felt like a major setback, he managed to turn things around for himself pretty quickly. Although he went to his hometown high school during his junior year, he asked his Aunt Rose if he could live with her during his senior year so he could attend Instituto

Abel in Niterói, just across a bridge from the capital city. She said yes as quickly as Chagas and Miriam had, and Ronaldo suddenly got a second chance to live in Rio de Janeiro. As usual, he studied hard and was accepted to the Universidade Federal Fluminense to study engineering.

RELATIONSHIPS CAN FAST-TRACK YOUR SUCCESS

Our relationships are the most significant factor in whether we'll reach the heights we aspire to, and they affect the amount of positive influence we can have on the future. "The quality of our relationships determines the quality of our lives—and this is not exclusive to romantic partnerships," says Esther Perel, psychotherapist and *New York Times* bestselling author. Our success is directly influenced by the company we keep, so developing strong relationships is one of the best ways to reach our most meaningful goals and make a meaningful contribution to the world. The more successful we are at whatever we set out to do, the greater the chance we'll have of making a lasting impact or leaving a legacy, whether it's for our family, our community, or the whole world.

While we often think of a legacy as a financial gift like bequeathing a significant amount of money to a university or creating an endowment fund, legacies aren't limited to philanthropy. Some of the most enduring contributions have been made by activists, scientists and people of faith like Marie Curie, Albert Einstein, Martin Luther King Jr., Mother Teresa, and Nelson Mandela. What you do or support can be anything meaningful to you that can make something better than it is now. That might be renovating a run-down playground, starting a local food bank, creating a public service that doesn't exist, or beautifying your street by planting flowers or trees. The legacies we can leave can be as unique as we are. But the one thing that people who make a lasting impact all have in common is that there were people in their lives who believed in them.

Having a "village" of good friends and associates helps us to optimize our talents and skills and accomplish more than we can on our own. When we develop a strong connection with someone, one plus one equals more than two—more than the sum of its parts. Relationships can help us develop our strengths, capitalize on opportunities and accelerate our progress. When Ronaldo applied for his first paid internship at Citibank, his application was immediately accepted because he'd been referred by a classmate who was an intern there. "Dari knew I was always first or second in my class," he says, "so when the bank was looking for new talent, she gave them my résumé without a second thought."

For him, this confirmed that relationships could make the difference between his goal to become financially successful and falling short. "So I decided that I would always treat everyone well because the people we meet can be barriers or they can be bridges," he says. "We never know when our paths will cross again. The world is round."

When Ronaldo was later hired by Banco Mercantil de São Paulo, he developed a strong relationship with his supervisor and made a point of meeting and interacting with one of the bank's owners, hoping to pave his way to become the youngest general manager the bank had ever had. Ronaldo says, "The owner said, 'Why do you think I'm going to make you the general manager? The other GMs are forty years old. You're only twenty-four.'" But that didn't discourage him. He continued racking up outstanding performance reviews and decided to get his MBA even though that was unusual for commercial bank managers at that time.

"The bank's owner was a big believer in formal education," he says, "so he was impressed that I was getting my MBA." He chuckles and flashes his million-dollar smile. "The fact that I nagged him and disturbed his peace until he finally gave me the GM position probably helped too."

Over the next several years, Ronaldo brought significant business and clients to the bank and his performance was always in the top tier. The financial sector was glamorous, he was making good money and getting nice bonuses and he loved helping clients achieve their financial dreams. But he didn't love the work itself, and he was starting to feel restless because he was twenty-nine and he'd set a goal of starting his own business by the time he was thirty. So he studied a variety of business sectors and thought about what type of company he wanted to start. "I always heard of people saying we should do what we love, but the only people I knew that loved what they did were doctors and my wife. Everyone else worked for the money, and I didn't want to be one of those people. I wanted to make a lot of money, but I definitely wanted to like my work."

A possible answer presented itself when Paulo Jia, one of Ronaldo's clients at the bank, invited him to start an optical sales company. He had reservations but the timing was right, so he used a few vacation days and drove to São Paulo to explore the opportunity. At first he and Paulo had very different thoughts about how the company should operate, and by the end of the second day of hashing things over without coming to an agreement, Ronaldo was ready to head home. But his wife, Daniela, urged him to stay one more day, and that's when Ronaldo and Paulo finally reached an agreement.

"I went back to the bank on Monday and resigned," Ronaldo

says. "My director and the bank owners said, 'Are you crazy? You can't quit your job. You have a very promising career at the bank.' But when I explained that starting a company was my dream and part of my life plan, they helped me to finance the business."

Starting General Optical turned out to be the first move on what would be a continually upward trajectory, but Ronaldo couldn't have climbed so high if his wife hadn't been totally on board. In addition to the financial risk, he had to live in São Paulo for two years without Daniela, who couldn't leave Rio because she was the market intelligence manager at SC Johnson. So she and their two-year-old son stayed in Rio and Ronaldo flew in on weekends. "Those were challenging years with plenty of difficulties," he says, "but Dani never stopped believing in me. She's been my biggest supporter all along."

Ronaldo's experience is in line with research that shows that people in loving relationships create more wealth. According to the Harvard Study of Adult Development, loving relationships with spouses, family members, and friends have a stronger correlation to financial success than intelligence, friendliness, economic standing, or our parents' education levels.

The study, which has tracked thirteen hundred students over the past eighty-six years, also found that people in close, supportive relationships are happier and healthier and tend to live longer than people who aren't. In fact, the participants' capacity for close relationships predicted how well they did in all aspects of their lives. (The original participants were men because Harvard was an all-male college when the study began, but Robert Waldinger, the study's current director and author of *The Good Life: Lessons from the World's Longest Scientific Study of Happiness*, has expanded the research to include the men's wives and children.) Some of the most compelling findings, summarized by Harvard research psychiatrist George Vaillant, include:

- Men who were close to one or more siblings earned $51,000 more a year than those who didn't have siblings or had poor relationships with them.
- Study participants who grew up in stable families earned $66,000 more a year than those who grew up in unstable homes.
- Men who reported having mothers who were warm made $87,000 more a year than those who described their mothers as uncaring.
- The fifty-eight participants with the highest scores for warm relationships earned nearly $150,000 more a year than the thirty-one who scored the lowest.

One of the study's most promising findings is that participants who didn't have close family relationships when they were young but formed warm relationships in midlife with friends, spouses, and children were happier and more successful in their later years than those who didn't develop close relationships in midlife. So, no matter what type of relationships you had when you were young, you can begin developing close ones now.

RELATIONSHIPS MAKE THE WORLD GO AROUND

Since the relationships we cultivate and the village we create play such a significant role in our ability to make a lasting impact, we can give ourselves an advantage by intentionally investing in existing relationships and developing new ones.

While networking has gotten a bad reputation, creating and maintaining strong connections is nothing like forging transactional relationships. It's just the opposite. Expanding our reach by meeting new people and developing genuine connections helps us to become better people and better leaders.

A Harvard research study showed that companies benefit when they're led by CEOs who have robust networks and even more so when their networks are diverse. The research team, led by Yiwei Fang, used BoardEx data to study more than a thousand CEOs of S&P 1500 firms for ten years, analyzing their personal and professional networks, and found that "CEOs with strong connections to people of different demographic backgrounds and skill sets created higher firm value."[12] Specifically, those diverse connections led to improved corporate innovations and diversified mergers and acquisitions.

A diversified social network is a key ingredient of company growth. And so is relationship-building itself. In a three-year study about the effects of networking on career success, researchers at the University of Erlangen-Nuremberg determined that networking is a "critical competency." H.G. Wolff and K. Moser studied 279 employed individuals and found that relationships that provide mutual benefits help us to "search for and secure employment opportunities, gain access to needed information or resources—especially on short notice—and obtain guidance, sponsorship, and social support."[3]

As my friend Ronaldo's experience beautifully illustrates, it's not money that makes the world go around. It's relationships. Ronaldo had the determination and initiative to create opportunities for himself, but without the people who believed in his dreams, his upward trajectory would have been slower and more difficult. Like the seventeenth century poet John Donne said, "No man is an island, entire of itself;

every man is a piece of the continent, a part of the main." Donne's words reflect the philosophical ideology that we all need to rely on others to survive and thrive; nobody is entirely self-sufficient. If you look into the backgrounds of people you admire or are inspired by, you'll see that there were one or more people in their village who helped them significantly. That doesn't diminish the value of their success. Their success means *more* because of the rich relationships they've cultivated and the sense of belonging that comes from being part of a supportive group.

If you're stopping yourself from creating or strengthening a connection because you're worried the other person might think you're selfishly motivated, consider how your knowledge, experience or other assets can benefit them. Great relationships are always two-way streets. If Ronaldo didn't have his bank clients' best interests at heart, Paulo Jia wouldn't have invited him to start General Optical together. As it was, the trust they'd fostered over the years helped them to grow GO into the second-largest eyewear sales company in Brazil in just four years.

The vast majority of professional and financial opportunities come from people in our network. Career consultants and outplacement specialists consider networking essential for success and estimate that people who effectively network get more than 70 percent of the most sought-after jobs. Having trustworthy relationships at work means you'll hear about positions that are opening up, pending layoffs and other insider news that may affect your job or give you an edge on advancement. Trust is one of the most valuable assets in all relationships, and it's built over time. To build it, you need to reach out, touch base and invest in the relationship. Connections built with trust are built to last. As these relationships develop we become interested in helping each other to reach goals and dreams, including by sharing knowledge and information.

Another benefit of building an extensive network is the huge net we can cast when we're looking for new opportunities. When Ronaldo left GO shortly after he and his partner sold their equity in the company, the main shareholder of another Brazilian eyewear company contacted him almost immediately. The shareholder had heard about how Ronaldo grew GO and wanted him to work his magic to rescue and revive Óticas Carol. The company had more than 150 franchise stores, but sixty of the franchisees were unhappy and planning to leave. Ronaldo was offered the CEO position, a six-figure salary and a substantial percentage of the company's equity. He accepted the offer to turn things around, and that's exactly what he did. Within eight years, the company grew to fourteen hundred stores and was attracting potential buyers. Óticas Carol was the market leader and Ronaldo was earning more than he'd ever dreamed he could make. That didn't make him complacent, though. When Óticas Carol sold part of the company to an investor, Ronaldo seized the opportunity to increase his percentage of the company's equity.

"Not long after that, I was comparing prices for a family vacation and I realized we could afford to go wherever we wanted to go and stay as long as we liked," Ronaldo says. "I had to stop for minute to take it in. I'd finally reached the goal I was working toward my whole life. It was funny because my nose had been to the grindstone for so long that it didn't sink in."

TOGETHER, WE CAN MAKE
THE WORLD BETTER

True to form, when the reality that Ronaldo had exceeded his financial goals *did* sink in, he decided that good wasn't good enough. "To be truly successful I needed to transform society, and I began looking for a way to do that," he says.

Since Óticas Carol sold eyewear, Ronaldo read a lot of reports about the market and the demographics that bought the brands they carried. In the process, he learned that 120 million Brazilians needed some type of correction lenses and 40 million of them had never had an eye exam. In addition, there were 7 million children who needed correction lenses, and many of *them* had never had an eye exam. "I remember thinking, 'How can we justify not helping them?'" he says. "So I decided we would be part of the solution by helping children to see." In 2015 the company started a project called Pequenos Olhares (Little Eyes) to offer deeply discounted glasses that could be paid for with a layaway plan. Parents could pay $2.50 a month, interest-free, for ten months, which made it a very affordable option.

The following year, Óticas Carol only accepted franchisees that understood the concept of the initiative. "We wanted people to recognize they had a social responsibility and be aligned with our purpose," Ronaldo says. "The franchisees who joined us understood that Pequenos Olhares is important to the business and also important for them on a personal level because by committing to helping others, we become better human beings ourselves."

"I know what it's like to need something and not be able to afford it," Ronaldo says. "When I was growing up, we didn't always have enough money for school supplies, let alone anything extra. But I had good eyesight, so I could read, and that gave me an advantage I didn't know I had at the time. Being able to give other kids that advantage means the world to me."

Years later, when Ronaldo joined Ri Happy, one of his first initiatives was to form a social impact committee to create an organized system for giving toys to children with disabilities and special needs and children who live in the most poverty-stricken parts of Brazil. The impact of the Ri Happy toys initiative has been so positive that Ronaldo is still part of the committee even though he resigned as CEO to explore new ventures.

Paying it forward is a practice that Ronaldo observed in many of the people he admired, including his grandparents and Chagas and Miriam. "There were a lot of things I didn't have as a kid, but I always had my family's support. My parents, grandparents, aunts and uncles all believed me when I said I would grow up to be successful. They didn't know how I would do it, and neither did I, but knowing that so many people were there to lend a hand when I asked for one made all the difference."

The relationships we have in childhood build our beliefs and affect our well-being and opportunities throughout life. So if we want to make a lasting impact, it's helpful to learn how our current views were formed. Since your childhood "village" influenced your perception of other people, the world, and life itself, exploring the ways those relationships affect how you see yourself today can reveal valuable information. Whether the input you received in childhood was positive or negative, your young mind accepted it as truth. You weren't experienced enough to know that what adults said might not accurately reflect who you were or who you could become. So your self-image and what you believe you're capable of accomplishing is directly connected to how your caregivers, siblings, teachers, and community saw you and how they showed their love or didn't. Once you know what's dimming your image of yourself, you can strip away the power of those influences. While you can't change what's already happened, you can use what you learn about your past to improve your relationships and increase your impact going forward.

By the time Ronaldo started seventh grade, his family had moved twenty times and his father's entrepreneurial history looked like a roller coaster track. When business was booming, they had the best. When it wasn't, they made do with what they had, sometimes living with Ronaldo's maternal or paternal grandparents. Ronaldo had set his own sights so high that every time his family experienced a setback, he became more frustrated. But when he had teenagers of his own, he began to see his father's entrepreneurial ups and downs from a different perspective. "Two things define my father's legacy," he says. "One is honesty. Honesty was non-negotiable. And the second was not giving up. Every time a business fell apart, my father picked up the pieces and started again. He did this at least thirty times. In retrospect, I could see that it was truly amazing."

Today, Ronaldo can see even more benefits from his childhood. If he'd been content with his school and his surroundings, he might not have dreamed of going to the naval school and wouldn't have had Chagas, Miriam, and Paulo as role models. Making new connections and expanding his network has been easy and fun for him partly because he'd changed schools so many times and always had to make new friends. "I didn't like it then, but now I see it was great practice at relationship-building," he says.

Ronaldo's childhood circumstances also gave him a chance to live with and learn from his grandparents, Chagas and

Miriam, and his Aunt Rose. Between his loving, supportive family members and the encouragement he received from his teachers, he believed in himself and his dreams.

Parents, family members, teachers and community members all influence whether children believe their dreams are possible and whether they see other people as fundamentally good or bad. It turns out that we need a village not only to raise a child but also to accomplish our goals and leave a legacy. Children who grow up in a culture where no one is left behind tend to become adults who believe people are innately good and helpful. They know their team has their back and are more likely to set the bar high and exceed their goals.

Sigmund Freud, neurologist and founder of psychoanalysis, theorized that our superego—the internal voice we hear as adults—is actually the internalized voices of our parents. So if we had supportive, positive parents and caregivers, we're more likely to have positive self-talk and healthy self-esteem.

Consider how the following statements heard during childhood can be internally repeated as adults:

- It's okay that you lost that match. You gave it your best, and your opponent was very good.
- Second place is the first loser.
- I'm sure you'll succeed in whatever you decide to do.
- You'll never amount to much.
- You have to dream big to achieve big things.
- Forget about those pipe dreams and make an honest living.

If the input you received when you were growing up was mostly judgmental, harsh or unforgiving, you've probably internalized some of that criticism and say those things to yourself. When a client has a highly critical internal voice, one of the first steps in therapy is to explore when the voice became so unaccepting and harsh and who spoke to them like that when they were children. Usually, we can trace the critical voice back to a parent, teacher or someone else from their community. Since harsh self-talk is typically the echo of a voice you heard in your formative years, it's important to identify the voice as not your own and systematically challenge it. Changing limiting beliefs is hard work, but it can be done.

Researchers have learned that when parents and other primary caregivers respond to a child's needs, the child develops a sense of security. When needs are not addressed, children become insecure. John Bowlby, a psychologist who did pioneering work about how children become attached to parents and caregivers, said that when babies know the people caring for them are dependable, they feel safe enough to explore the world. With this upbringing, they also tend to see people as generally dependable, predictable, and safe. So if your first relationships were loving, secure, and affirming like Ronaldo's, you have a good foundation for thriving as an adult. It's not a direct cause-and-effect dynamic, but you certainly had a head start. For example, if your parents had a happy marriage and good relationships with relatives, friends and neighbors, it's probably easy for you to develop healthy relationships characterized by interdependence, commitment, trust, satisfaction and positive emotions.[4]

On the other hand, if you grew up in an ultra-competitive family or community where one person's gain was another's loss, you may believe people are innately self-centered, aggressive, and even cutthroat. Understandably, children who weren't nurtured or supported or grew up in unstable or violent homes often have more obstacles to overcome in adulthood. If this is true for you and you could redesign your childhood, wouldn't you make sure "little you" had nurturing people all around? Wouldn't you surround yourself with emotionally stable people who embrace you for who you are? Wouldn't you want people in your life who had encouraging words and lovingly challenged you to be and do your best?

Do you see where I'm going with this? You have the opportunity to do this *now*. You can design your future and make a positive difference by choosing the people you surround yourself with *today and tomorrow*. Since the relationships you have today affect your success, health, and happiness, developing a supportive village is the best way to reach your goals, both big and small. By reviewing what you appreciated and what you didn't in relationships you had during the first eighteen years of your life, you can gain insight into the relationships you want to develop. But to move toward your idea of success, insight isn't enough. Progress takes action, so the exercises and steps in the upcoming chapters will help you to use what you discover to improve your relationships with others and with yourself. It's not your fault if your parents weren't supportive or worse, but if your past is making it hard for you to create the future you want, you're the only one who can minimize the negative effects. You can't change your past, but you *can* change your future.

———————

IN BRIEF

- Your relationships are the most significant factor in whether you'll reach the heights you aspire to, and they affect the amount of positive influence you have on the future.
- Your success is directly influenced by the company you keep, so developing strong relationships is one of the best ways to reach your most meaningful goals and make a lasting impact.
- When you develop a strong connection with someone, one plus one equals more than two.
- It's not money that makes the world go around. It's relationships.
- You need a village, not only to raise a child, but also to accomplish your goals, make a lasting impact or leave a legacy.
- To move toward your idea of success, insight isn't enough. Progress takes action.
- You can't change your past, but you *can* change your future.

––––––––––

In Chapter Two, you'll find out how to close the gap between who you are and who you aspire to be.

CHAPTER 2

PURPOSE MAKES LIFE MORE MEANINGFUL

When Launchcode's CEO rang in the New Year on January 1, 2020, he was the dictionary definition of success. Together with his co-founder, Alberio Bathory-Frota, he had grown the start-up into two businesses, a full-service development company and a security product company that validated more than 160 million identities throughout the world, all in the span of fifteen years. My brother also had a happy marriage and two wonderful kids in middle school. He was living the proverbial American dream. But something was missing—he wasn't as passionate about his work as he used to be.

Alberio's days were consumed by daily operations, and the constant demands of running two international companies were steadily robbing him of his energy and enthusiasm. Because of the long days, he was also missing his kids' sports activities and special occasions. "I was grateful I could provide a good life for my family and that Launchcode and Patronscan were helping to make the world a better place with innovative technology, but I was starting to wonder if all the sacrifices were really worth it," he says. He didn't have time to dwell on that, though, because Patronscan was about to launch a pilot program in Alberta, Canada, for a company that owned hundreds of liquor stores throughout the country. And to stay on top of the operational demands of running both companies and prepare for the launch, he was working nights and weekends.

In Alberta's capital city Edmonton, thefts at liquor stores had risen from 3,588 in 2017 to 11,696 in 2019, and robberies involving violence or the threat of violence had nearly doubled in the same time. The pilot program's objective was to find out if requiring customers to scan their IDs before they were allowed into the stores would lower those numbers. As it turned out, thefts at stores using Patronscan *immediately* dropped 94 percent and robberies were eliminated altogether. It was a huge success. But the celebration was short-lived.

The publicity attracted the attention of Alberta's information and privacy commissioner and she launched a public investigation to determine if Patronscan's technology was in compliance with information and privacy laws. "News anchors and reporters all over Alberta picked up the story about the investigation and questioned our company's integrity, which made some companies reluctant to do business with us," Alberio says. Instead of reaping the rewards of a job well done, Alberio was spending precious time defending a product that was already compliant with privacy laws around the world.

After a twenty-one-month investigation, the commission said liquor stores could continue to collect customers' information so they could stop people with prior offenses from entering the store and share crime-related information with the police. Today, liquor stores in two Canadian provinces use Patronscan to enhance safety for employees and patrons by eliminating violent robberies. So the project was finally a success—something the company's CEO could be rightfully proud of.

But Alberio wasn't feeling it. Instead of being rejuvenated by this latest victory, he just felt drained by the effort it had taken. And adding insult to injury, when COVID-19 shut down the hospitality industry, Patronscan lost more than 80 percent of its revenue.

"I knew we might go under, and I started thinking a lot about what that would mean," Alberio says. "After years of running the company, it was part of my identity. If we went bankrupt, it would mean that I'm a failure, right? It was such a big hit that it made me ask, what *is* my sense of purpose? What am I supposed to be doing?"

The existential crisis gave him an opportunity to question everything about his identity, down to: "At my core, who am I?" He decided to hire a coach, and the extensive clarity process he completed allowed him to see that the work he was doing was good but it wasn't good for *him*. "What I really have big passion about is the creative process," he says. "I love collaborating with people at ground level to build organizations and create new products and solutions. As a traditional CEO, I wasn't very involved in the creation process anymore."

His self-reflection and soul-searching helped him to see that many of his executive responsibilities didn't align with his purpose. "I realized that I wanted to continue to lead our vision and mission and be involved in the ideation phase of products and new ventures because I'm passionate about those things and they're what I do best," he says. "And instead of hiring a new CEO, I also decided to develop a leadership team to handle all the other executive responsibilities. With a team that's greater than the sum of its parts, we can create a healthy, collaborative culture that makes the company more successful long term. And I also really like the inherent humility that's required for a strong leadership team that emphasizes the team and shared mission over any single individual."

I've been cheering on my younger brother and applauding his accomplishments every step of the way, from leaving a secure job to pursue his entrepreneurial dreams to growing the company into the global influencer that it is today. But when he got clear about what mattered most to him and took action to close the gap between his reality and his purpose, that called for a standing ovation.

GET CLEAR ABOUT YOUR PURPOSE

Imagine that when you wake up tomorrow, you're so inspired that you can't wait to get up and get to work. Try to picture what your day would look like from beginning to end. What would you do? Where would you do it? Who would you do it with?

My brother's story shows that high performers earning a good income don't always feel successful. The commonly accepted definitions of success are the achievement of a favorable or desired outcome and the attainment of wealth, favor or eminence. Neither definition says anything about living by our own values or pursuing our life purpose, and the second definition is at the core of why so many people feel like they're *not* succeeding: *How can I say I'm successful if I'm not wealthy?*

I'm proposing a new definition of success based on of what I've learned from research and my experience with clients. According to this definition, success is becoming the best version of yourself by pursuing a purpose that's meaningful to you. Because self-discovery and self-improvement are ongoing and your purpose can continue to evolve, there's no finish line, but you can continually narrow the gap between who you are and who you aspire to be.

Who You Are ——— Who You Aspire to Be

The current you is the one living in the real world. It's not the curated version that you publicly display or the edited version you post on social media. It's who you are, as you are.

Who you aspire to be is the person you're working toward becoming. You can think of it as the upgraded version, complete with all the personal improvements you want to make.

When you consider the person you aspire to be, it can be a little daunting to see how big the gap is right now, but you can cover the distance faster than you may think.

The formula is to identify and begin pursuing a purpose that's bigger than you—something that helps others—and then invite your village to join you. This will position you to make a meaningful impact and provide you with countless opportunities to learn and grow.

Getting clear about your purpose will also make it easier to see which relationships are working in your favor and which ones should be reevaluated. When I started writing this book, I swore I wasn't going to use the word *purpose* because it gets tossed into every pseudo-philosophical conversation I hear. But there's a reason *purpose* has become the word of the day. There isn't another English word that sums it up so well. (Believe me—I tried to find one.) So I'll use the "p" word interchangeably with *vision, mission, calling, passion* and other words that don't set off my cliché detector. Whatever we call it, if you're not doing what you're passionate about, the gap between who you are and who you want to be is probably pretty big. Not only that, but the incongruence can cause an enormous amount of stress.

As Emily Esfahani Smith says in *The Power of Meaning: Crafting a Life That Matters*, "We all need a far-reaching goal that motivates us, serves as the organizing principle of our lives, and drives us to make a contribution to the world."[1] Having a purpose is a pillar of a meaningful life and it doesn't have to be daunting. Ideally, your purpose will be simple, attainable, relevant, and in tune with your talents.

To make your life more meaningful and live your definition of success, take the steps to continually move toward your purpose. When Alberio clarified that he's most passionate about using his creativity and experience to help others build new companies and innovative products and solutions, he knew he had to share some of his executive responsibilities even though being the CEO had been a central part of his identity for years. Making these types of changes isn't easy, but if you define what success means to you and figure out what your purpose is, that clarity will give you wings.

Exercise: Find Your Reason for Being

If you don't already know your purpose, try using the Japanese concept *ikigai*—"a reason for being." You find your *ikigai* (pronounced ick-ee-guy) by aligning what you love with what you're good at, what the world needs and what you can be paid for.

To enhance your clarity, ask:

1. What do I love?
2. What am I good at?
3. What does the world need?
4. What can I be paid for?

Another way to figure out what you're inspired to do is to think about how you can use your passion and talents to help others and contribute something meaningful to the world. What can you improve? What types of problems can you solve? What type of legacy do you want to leave? Uri Levine, founder of the GPS navigation application Waze, explores this approach in *Fall in Love with the Problem, Not the Solution: A Handbook for Entrepreneurs.* Finding a problem to fall in love with is yet another way to find purpose.

There's a general consensus that at the end of our lives, we have more regrets about what we didn't do than about what we did do. If you fast-forward to the end of your life, what will you regret not doing? When people look back at their lives, their number one regret is that they lived according to what other people or society expected of them instead of how they *wanted* to live. Please don't let that regret be yours.

Having a meaningful reason to live helps you close the gap between who you are and who you aspire to be, which will make you happier and more fulfilled. Equally important, if you're not intentionally moving toward a more meaningful life, it's hard to tell if the relationships you're having are supporting your life goals or working against them. And since your relationships can be the most significant factor in whether you succeed, you want to make sure they're helping you to progress and not holding you back. But you may not be able to determine that until you clarify your purpose.

Being clear about your purpose also gives you strength and makes you more resilient, especially when the work is boring or difficult. When you focus on making a positive difference, the hard times become easier because the sacrifices have meaning. And when you feel like quitting, having strong relationships will make it easier to stay motivated and push forward.

FINDING MEANING GIVES US HOPE

We all have an idea of what's most meaningful to us, and most people have at least a few things they don't want to regret. But figuring out what we want to contribute to the world isn't always so obvious. And if we don't think we have something worthwhile to offer, we won't notice all the possibilities that exist for us. This was the case with my client, George. He had such a low opinion of himself that he didn't recognize his abilities and strengths and so he didn't think he had any choice but to keep doing what he was doing. Day after day he'd drag himself to work, and night after night he'd zone out in front of the TV with a six-pack.

George is the same age as Alberio—they even have the same birth date—so I couldn't help wondering how different George's life would be if he'd grown up in a supportive family like my brother, sister, and I had. It was yet another reminder of the uphill road faced by people who had traumatic childhoods. The toxic statements George heard from his mother were playing on an endless loop in his mind. When he said, "I'm a piece of crap," I wasn't surprised to learn that his mother repeatedly told him that when he was growing up.

"I consider you a contributing member of society," I said.

He grunted and shook his head. "But I'm not."

"Do you pay income tax? Yes. Are you on unemployment insurance? No, you're not. Do you vandalize or break things that belong to other people? No. What do you do? You drive kids to school so they can get an education and you coach a kids' soccer team. Of course you contribute."

"Anybody can do those things," he said. "It's not like they need *me*."

Children who suffer verbal and physical abuse often have a difficult time contributing to society, so George's contributions were impressive, but he had a hard time seeing that. When I told him that kids who are abused are more likely to be abusive adults, he was surprised, but it didn't make him feel any better about himself, even when I explained that he'd successfully broken the cycle of violence.

I thought George was inspiring, but he sure didn't see himself that way. He was so sad that before we could work on any lasting changes, we had to work on his relationship with himself and with the people closest to him. His father repeatedly "borrowed" money and didn't pay it back. His girlfriend, who hadn't paid her share of the rent or spent a dime on groceries in years, was controlling and manipulative. His sister, who lived just a few miles away, said he drank too much to be a good role model for his nephews and wouldn't let him visit. The list went on and on. As dismal as George's life felt to him, I knew he could turn things around if he could see himself more objectively—the way *I* saw him. But he didn't believe he deserved a better life, and he couldn't imagine being able to make a lasting contribution. More than once he said, "I don't want to kill myself. I just want this life to be over."

In *Man's Search for Meaning*, when Viktor Frankl recounts his experience in Nazi concentration camps, he explains that if prisoners lost their reason to live—their why—they rejected all help or encouragement with statements like "I have nothing to expect from life anymore."[2] Frankl writes, "What was really needed was a fundamental change in our attitude toward life. We had to teach the despairing men that it did not really matter what we expected from life, but rather what life expected from us."

I wanted George to discover what life might expect from him, but he wasn't able to look for the answer to that question while he was dealing with so many external burdens. So first we worked on setting better boundaries with his father and standing up to his mooching girlfriend, but he didn't give himself credit for the progress he was making, and even though he said he wouldn't take his own life, he was having suicidal thoughts every day. But he still wanted to try to make his life better, so he kept coming to therapy and we kept working on his self-worth and talking about how he could spend more time doing the things that made life feel worthwhile to him.

I was pleased with the progress he was making, but one day, instead of actively engaging in the work we were doing, he was totally resigned. It seemed like he'd lost hope, and it scared me.

"George, I need you to do me a favor," I said as our session came to an end.

He looked a little surprised. "What is it?"

"I've never given you homework, but I need you to stay alive for our session next week. I need you to not kill yourself before Monday."

"I can do that," he said. "No big deal."

He sounded sincere, but I worried all weekend.

On Monday morning, as I waited for him to join my Zoom room, I was afraid he wouldn't show up. It wasn't until I saw his face that I realized I'd been holding my breath. He was actually smiling a little too, and when I asked him how he was doing, he got right to the point.

"You know how my sister said I drink too much?"

I nodded.

"She's probably right," he said.

For the first time, he was asking me to work with him on his addiction—a huge step.

Less than a month later, he checked himself into a rehab program. Before he went in, he called me. "I want you to know that it's because of you that I'm going to rehab," he said. "When you asked me not to kill myself, I thought, *Man, I gotta do something.*"

When George finished the program a few months later, I didn't recognize him. He was a different person. He said he had half his life ahead of him and had committed to staying sober. He enrolled in a program to get his high school diploma and said he was thinking of applying for assistant soccer coach positions at nearby middle schools. Once George knew he wanted to help kids avoid making the same mistakes he'd made, his whole life looked different to him. Once he knew what his purpose was, his life had meaning. *He had hope.* Now he could appreciate what he'd accomplished and was excited about planning a bright future. And he finally realized that he deserved to have better relationships, so he broke up with his girlfriend and stopped lending his father money. Every time I see him, he has good news about what he's accomplishing and the plans he's making.

MOVE TOWARD YOUR PURPOSE

People who are intentionally pursuing their life purpose tend to agree with statements like "I have a sense of direction and purpose in life," "I enjoy making plans for the future and working to make them a reality," and "Some people wander aimlessly through life, but I'm not one of them."

People who haven't identified a meaningful purpose are more likely to agree with statements like "I live life one day at a time and don't really think about the future," "I don't have a good sense of what it is I'm trying to accomplish in life," "I sometimes feel as if I've done all there is to do in life," and "My daily activities often seem trivial and unimportant to me." These statements are from a section on "Pursuit of Meaningful Goals and Sense of Purpose" in the Ryff Scales of Psychological Well-Being.

Once George had a meaningful reason to live, he began valuing himself and was able to distance himself from his dysfunctional relationships. He was also able to strengthen the relationships he had with people who supported his dream to help kids succeed. Today, George is happy, optimistic, and even committed to getting healthy. He's walking every day, rain or shine, he's replaced beer with sparkling water, and he's stopped calling potato chips *vegetables.*

Becoming rich or famous can be a purpose, but if you reach that summit and the journey has been only about you, will you feel like you have nothing left to expect from life? If that seems likely, it might be more inspiring to focus on how your fame or fortune can benefit others and make the world a little better. A research study led by Roy F. Baumeister at Florida State University shows that we get longer-lasting satisfaction when we strive for purpose and meaning than when we seek happiness.[3]

When your purpose is good for you *and* good for others, it's a win-win. "For me, it's about making a positive difference in the world and having a meaningful impact with my family, friends, and community," Alberio says. "The more I work on myself, the stronger my inner circle becomes, and that, by default, increases the impact that I can have."

Tips for Identifying Your Purpose

1. Think long-term. Choose a purpose that doesn't have a finish line so you can continually become a better version of yourself.
2. We're all in this together, so try using the *ikigai* approach to choose a purpose that combines what you love with what you're good at, what the world needs, and what you can be paid for.
3. Review your personal history. Your purpose may be inspired by something you've observed or experienced.

Exercise: Review Your Personal History

Was there a sport or hobby that defined you, helped you gain confidence, or just made you happy? If so, you may want to coach or mentor kids who are interested in the same sport or hobby.

Did you play the unofficial role of mediator or peacekeeper in your family? If so, your purpose might be to play this role in your community.

The objective of this life review is to look for a theme.

For each decade of your life, starting at age ten, answer the following questions:

- What was I doing?
- Where did I live?
- Who were the five most important people to me at this time? (friends and family)
- What were my main accomplishments during this time? (Instead of listing everything you achieved, focus on the accomplishments you found most important and relevant at the time or in hindsight.)
- What was your biggest disappointment during this decade?
- What were your interests?
- Choose five words that best describe you in this age bracket.

For each decade, use a separate sheet of paper so you can put the pages in consecutive order and review your whole life while looking for common themes.

My friend Veronica found her purpose while she was raising her son, who has dyslexia and attention-deficit/hyperactivity disorder (ADHD). As an adult, these incurable conditions still challenge Matheus, but thanks to the work Veronica did for him when he was young, he now works for an investment company and is thriving. During Matheus's childhood, Veronica constantly advocated for him with teachers and school administrators because no adaptations were available for kids with learning disabilities in Fortaleza, Brazil, at the time. When she couldn't find an expert to help Matheus, she became one herself. She learned everything she could about his learning disabilities and used that knowledge to find appropriate schools with environments that supported her son's learning and personal growth. He attended a specialized high school in the US and did so well he was able to attend a mainstream university there. When Veronica saw how her knowledge and advocacy transformed her son's life, she made it her mission to help other families to improve their kids' lives and launched a consulting service. Today, she teaches how to positively parent kids with dyslexia and ADHD and also offers workshops and private coaching.

Another friend's purpose is to help refugee families to immigrate because he believes that when people are given a fair chance, they thrive. He believes this because his own family immigrated to Canada when he was a child and his parents were given the opportunity to earn a living and received a lot of encouragement and support from their community. Today, he's a lawyer and he credits his success to the opportunities Canada offered and to the people who helped his family when they were refugees.

Both of these friends have life purposes they can work on forever. And in both cases, their personal experiences showed them what the world needed and helped them to discover and strengthen abilities and talents they could use to help others.

As Ai Weiwei, one of my favorite artists and activists, says: "The refugee crisis isn't about refugees. It's about us."
As you consider what your purpose might be, keep in mind:

- It doesn't have to be fancy or grandiose. It's about doing something that's meaningful to *you*.
- It should be consistent with your values and talents.
- It can be as simple as: Treat all human beings with respect. I have a client who decided he was going to be nice and smile at everyone he encountered. His days became full of meaning because he felt the positive impact he had on others.
- It can be about being the best person you can be in all your roles and relationships—parent, partner, sibling, child, friend, neighbor, colleague.

"What would you do if you knew you could not fail?" a question often attributed to US First Lady Eleanor Roosevelt, is a great question to ask. Choosing a meaningful mission will not only help you become the best version of yourself, but it will also dramatically improve your state of mind, enhance your health and happiness and may even contribute to a longer life. And all of these improvements can also help you to have more fulfilling relationships. Researchers have found that people who are pursuing a meaningful purpose are happier and healthier than people who are primarily seeking pleasure. In one study, the purpose-driven participants even had more active immune systems than those seeking happiness. An active, strong immune system can decrease inflammation, fight viral infections, and may reduce our chances of cardiovascular, neurodegenerative and other life-threatening diseases. The people pursuing happiness, on the other hand, had lab results that were similar to the results of people who have high anxiety or are under a lot of stress.[4]

So doing good and feeling good don't affect us the same way even though they both generate positive emotions. Pursuing happiness for the sake of happiness isn't as powerful or productive as pursuing something meaningful that makes us happy. The difference may sound subtle, but the results are profoundly different.

Exercise: Hindsight Can Reveal Your Purpose

Another way to gain insight into your purpose is to imagine you're eighty years old and writing your memoir or telling your life story to your grandkids:

- What do you want to brag about having done?
- What contributions do you want to have made to others?
- What regrets do you not want to have?
- What would you have done if you had known you couldn't fail?

If you want to "look back" from the very end of your life, you can imagine your funeral:

- Who would you want to be there?
- What would you like them to say?
- How do you want people to remember you?
- What would you like your urn or gravestone to say?

———————

The fastest way to start closing the gap between who you are now and who you aspire to be is to fully commit to your purpose, make a plan with measurable goals to pursue it, and enrich the relationships that will support your progress. George still doesn't think of himself as a success, but he is absolutely succeeding because every day he's narrowing the gap between what his life is like today and what he wants to create tomorrow.

TO CONNECT AND INSPIRE, SHARE YOUR PURPOSE

There's a widespread belief that sharing our goals can help us to achieve them. I think that's true, but with some clarifications. If you share your dreams with people who support and constructively challenge you, they can help you to make them come true. But if you share these inspirations with people who have a lot of limiting beliefs or tend to be negative, their input can be discouraging and may even slow your progress. A 2020 study published in the *Journal of Applied Psychology* supports sharing intentions with "the right people," which the researchers defined as those who "have a higher status and those with more prestige and respect."[5] H.J. Klein, the study's lead researcher, says, "Contrary to what you may have heard, in most cases you get more benefit from sharing your goal than if you don't—as long as you share it with someone whose opinion you value. You want to be dedicated and unwilling to give up on your goal, which is more likely when you share that goal with someone you look up to." So share your purpose and goals with people you respect and people who have values similar to yours.

Sharing your purpose is also a wonderful way to inspire other people to think about what their purpose is, and it will help you connect with more people who want you to succeed. When my friend Andrea LaRochelle trademarked the term "Find the Good" (FTG), I couldn't wait to hear all about it. Andrea's a family mediator with extensive experience working with high-conflict individuals. She helps divorcing parents shift their focus from themselves to their children so that they can make decisions that put their kids first. Not an easy day at the office, right? No matter how effective someone is in this line of work or how rewarding it is, working through one conflict after another can be exhausting. So, to prevent compassion fatigue, Andrea made a conscious choice to find the good in everything—in the small miracles of the day, in the small wins, in the beauty of nature.

"Find the Good means something different to everyone," she says. "Life can be hard, messy, and unpredictable. Through those difficult times, there can also be good—but you have to look for it. And once you start looking, that's when the magic happens. Find the good."

Today, hundreds of people in Calgary, Alberta, have FTG swag and wear it proudly. During the pandemic, it was a way to rebel against the bad news we were bombarded with every day. Finding the good gave us hope during a scary and lonely time, and it enriched the conversations we had. Instead of talking about COVID-19 or the day's news, we talked about our values, and when we talk about what we treasure, we learn a lot about each other. When we have these types of conversations, we find out whose core values are aligned with ours and discover who else is exploring subjects and ideas that are meaningful to us.

Research studies on the benefits of living a purposeful life are relatively new, but the wisdom to find meaning and live on our own terms has been around for a long time:

"He who has a why to live for can bear almost any how."
—Friedrich Nietzsche, philosopher

"The mystery of human existence lies not in just staying alive, but in finding something to live for."
—Fyodor Dostoyevsky, novelist

"It's not enough to have lived. We should be determined to live for something."
—Winston Churchill, former British prime minister

"My mission in life is not merely to survive but to thrive and to do so with some passion, some compassion, some humor, and some style."
—Maya Angelou, poet and civil rights activist

"Fight for the things that you care about, but do it in a way that will lead others to join you."
—Ruth Bader Ginsburg, former associate justice of the Supreme Court of the United States

Because all of these people lived by values that were meaningful to them, they were able to make significant contributions to the world. And we can do that too.

Choosing to live your best life, to be helpful to others no matter what, to find the good—all these are amazing ways to make a positive difference. And it's easier to do when your purpose is clear and you surround yourself with people who also are committed to creating a better future for themselves and others. These people will encourage you to keep striving and you'll do the same for them. David McClelland, Harvard researcher and social psychologist, found that the people we habitually associate with determine as much as 95 percent of our success or failure. *Ninety-five percent.* So if you're sincere about moving toward your inspired vision, being selective about your relationships isn't just a good idea—it's essential.

Pursuing your purpose isn't always going to be blue skies and smooth sailing, so you need friends who will remind you that it's worth it and that *you're* worth it. If they're on board with your mission, they'll encourage you to stay on track despite disappointments and setbacks. When my client Michelle found out that only a small fraction of the money she donated to support refugees from Ukraine was making it to the families, she was devastated. Her purpose is to help victims of large-scale violence, and she's passionate about it because she grew up in a war zone and her home was destroyed by a bomb. She was so upset about the organization she'd given the donation to that she wanted to abandon her mission, but her friends wouldn't let her lose hope.

If her friends hadn't been aligned with her purpose, they could have said, "Here you're trying to help and people are taking advantage of you. Why bother?" Instead, they helped her connect with honest and successful humanitarian efforts around the world and taught her how to vet organizations so she wouldn't get scammed again. They acknowledged that, yes, some people are scammers and will take advantage of catastrophes, but they also reminded her that those people don't define humanity. In Michelle's most difficult hour, it wasn't her grit or determination that kept her going. It was the friends who were aligned with her purpose. One of the fastest, most effective ways to achieve your purpose is to create enriching connections.

IN BRIEF

- Success is being the best version of yourself while pursuing a purpose that's meaningful to you.
- Because self-discovery and self-improvement are ongoing and a purpose that makes a lasting impact can continue to evolve, there's no finish line. But you can continually narrow the gap between your current reality and your vision for tomorrow.
- Getting clear about your purpose will make it easier to see which relationships are working in your favor and which ones should be reevaluated.
- The incongruence between what you're doing and what you wish you were doing causes an enormous amount of stress.
- To determine your purpose, try using the Japanese concept *ikigai*—"a reason for being." You find your *ikigai* by aligning what you love with what you're good at, what the world needs and what you can be paid for.
- When people look back at their lives, their number one regret is that they lived according to what other people or society expected of them instead of how they *wanted* to live.

- Not only will choosing a meaningful mission help you become the best version of yourself, but it will also dramatically improve your state of mind, enhance your health and happiness, and may even contribute to a longer life.
- Pursuing happiness for the sake of happiness isn't as powerful or productive as pursuing something meaningful that makes you happy.
- If you share your dreams with people who support and constructively challenge you, they can help you to make them come true.

In Chapter Three, you'll learn how creating a village can help you to make a lasting impact.

CHAPTER 3

IT TAKES A VILLAGE TO LEAVE A LEGACY

66 "For me, making a lasting impact means doing work that makes me happy and being the best person I can be," says Daniela Castro, director of market intelligence and innovation at Heineken, Brazil. As a young girl Daniela was impressed that her father, a commercial sales director, enjoyed his work, had the freedom to do whatever he wanted, and always seemed to be doing something to help someone in one way or another. "He taught me that we all have an opportunity and a responsibility to make the world a little better while we're here and it's a lot easier to do that if we enjoy our life, including the work we do." Daniela's definition of making a lasting impact has been guiding her decisions ever since.

After earning a business degree, she was hired as a trainee at Banco Nacional. She liked the job, but when Coca-Cola offered her a position in the marketing department, it was too enticing to refuse even though the salary was lower. She says, "It was the right move to make because I found my lifelong passions at Coca-Cola—market intelligence and consumer insight—and within a year I was making more than I'd made at the bank and having a lot more fun."

The office location and prestige weren't bad either. "At the time, Coca-Cola had a lot of status and everyone wanted to work there," she says. "The Rio de Janeiro office was in a beautiful building in Botafogo with a stunning view of Guanabara Bay." But what Daniela didn't appreciate—the office politics and her supervisor's management style—took the fun out of the job. So when she was offered a marketing services manager position at SC Johnson, she accepted. Although the SC Johnson location was anything but picturesque and her commute included Vulture Road, appropriately named for the abundance of road kill, "I found my happy place there," Daniela says, "and I also found myself." It was there that Daniela began to develop her leadership skills. "My supervisor, the chief marketing officer, was a fabulous leader," she says. "Ana Maria was the opposite of my boss at Coca-Cola. She was a good team leader, super-accessible, spoke to me directly and taught me things that I didn't know. She was always encouraging and also motivated me to do better and be better, and that's exactly what I wanted. I looked up to Ana Maria. She wasn't an official mentor, but she was someone I wanted to mirror, and she became a benchmark for me."

Ana Maria always gave her team recognition for the work they did, and that paved Daniela's way to promotion. "I earned my master's degree in marketing and had three children while working there. After I came back from one of my maternity leaves, I got promoted to start a new position," she says. "I was never punished for starting a family. SC Johnson was very aligned with my values and I loved it there."

But after five years, she missed working with market intelligence and consumer insight, so she asked to change positions.

"When Ana Maria received my request, she told me the market intelligence path didn't lead to a chief marketing officer position, which is what people with master's degrees typically want. That made me reconsider, but after talking with her about my passion and the trade-offs of not pursuing a CMO position, I was sure that following my heart was the right way to go."

Being on Ana Maria's team helped Daniela to gain more clarity about her career trajectory, and following her heart paid off big time. Not long after she left SC Johnson, she became consumer strategy and insights director of PepsiCo and eventually became senior director of consumer strategy and insights for all of Latin America. "I learned more in my first few years than I would have thought was possible," Daniela says. "And then I got the best surprise of my career. Patricia, a friend I'd made at Coca-Cola, was hired by Pepsi and became my new boss."

Daniela and Patricia had stayed in touch over the years, and in addition to being a friend, she was a mentor. "I admire Patricia because she's very good at looking at the big picture and has a balanced point of view," Daniela says. "When we connected, we'd often talk about our careers and brainstorm the best ways to move forward, and she was always willing to give me her honest opinion."

At Pepsi, it was Patricia who pointed out Daniela's talent for developing teams. "She saw this quality in me that I hadn't perceived in myself. That helped me to fully embrace the role of team developer, and now that I'm at Heineken, building strong, effective teams is one of the most rewarding things I do. Even though it's been years since Patricia and I have worked together, she'll always be part of my village."

Associating with people who make you better is like playing a game or sport with a better player—it raises your own game. People you spend time with influence what you talk about, how you behave, and even what you value. Way back in the first century AD, the Greek philosopher Epictetus said, "The key is to keep company only with people who uplift you, whose presence calls forth your best."

Fast-forward to the twenty-first century:

> "A mirror reflects a man's face, but what he is really like is shown by the kind of friends he chooses."
> —Colin Powell, former US secretary of state

> "One of the most effective things you can do to build better habits is to join a culture where your desired behavior is the normal behavior. Your culture sets your expectation for what is 'normal.' Surround yourself with people who have the habits you want to have yourself. You'll rise together."
> —James Clear, author of Atomic Habits

To give yourself the best advantage, surround yourself with people who cheer you on and celebrate your success. Ideally, they'll also be good influences, since the more time you spend with someone, the more similar you're likely to become.

The effects can be more dramatic in a group because everyone's values tend to shift toward the group norm. So it's important to look at the norms in your groups and consider whether you're aligned with them and whether they're aligned with the impact you want to make. Don't leave this to chance, because just like people in your past shaped who you are today, the company you're keeping today is influencing who you'll be tomorrow. So develop and strengthen relationships with people who expect a lot from themselves and will expect a lot from you. If you want to be better and do better, associate with people you admire.

For Daniela, associating with people who had high expectations of her began with her own family. "My parents implicitly believed that I could do anything I set my mind to," she says, "so I've always set the bar high for myself. I sought out positions at multinational companies because I wanted to work with people who held themselves to high standards. In those environments, we all grow and thrive."

INVEST IN YOUR VILLAGE

Melody and Peter both graduated from Ivy League universities and wanted to head NGOs as fast as they could. But they also wanted to have kids. After a lot of negotiating, they made a deal to take turns being the primary caregiver. When their twins were born, Melody would be the primary caregiver for two years and then it would be Peter's turn. But when the time came, Peter wouldn't hold up his end of the deal. Melody came to see me because she and Peter were at an impasse and had basically stopped talking to each other. "I'm happy he loves his job and that he's already in line for a promotion," she said, "but after two years of picking up toys and drowning in diapers, it's my turn to go back to work and he refuses to even talk about it." She shook her head. "I still can't believe he's doing this."

Up to that point, she and Peter had been in a friendly race to success that motivated both of them to accomplish more. The competition served as career fuel, and they'd always cheered each other on and celebrated each other's success. "Competing made us better," Melody said. "But now he acts like his dreams are the only ones that matter. I mean, I'm happy that he's inspired about what he's doing, and I'm proud he's doing so well, but . . ." Her eyes filled with tears and she reached for a tissue. "I shouldn't have agreed to move to Calgary. If we were in Toronto, I'd have my family and my friends to help out."

Melody explained that she'd worked for a nonprofit in Toronto and had been surrounded by people who supported her dream to run an NGO and possibly start one herself one day. She loved her job, she and Peter were happy and they were saving money to start a family. A few months after they found out she was pregnant, Peter was offered a director's position at an NGO in Calgary. "I didn't want to move," she said, "but the job meant a lot to him, so I agreed to go."

She said raising the twins was all-consuming and she wasn't getting much help from Peter, so she didn't have a chance to make new friends or catch up very often with her old ones. "It's bad enough that he's not keeping our bargain. When he's home, he's constantly checking his messages and scrolling through his phone."

Melody told me that she wanted to make her marriage work but that it was hard not to feel frustrated when Peter was pursuing his dream and hers was on hold. Instead of closing the gap between where she was and where she wanted to be, she felt that the gap was getting bigger every day. "This is not what I pictured for myself," she said. "I have things I want to accomplish, just like Peter does. Why should I have to be the one who stays home just because I'm the mother?"

She wasn't comfortable with enrolling the twins in day care or hiring a nanny who was a total stranger, so she thought her only options were to keep doing what she was doing or pack up the kids and go back to Toronto.

As we looked at what was contributing to her despair, it was clear that being disconnected from her closest relationships—including her marriage—was a major factor. So before we talked about making big decisions like moving back to Toronto, I wanted her to strengthen her relationships.

We know from research and everyday life that people who have strong relationships are healthier and happier than people who don't. And that's true in good times and in bad. Jeffrey Hall, a professor of communication studies at the University of Kansas, says that if your goal is to prevent the health hazards of loneliness, it's essential to have at least one close relationship in your life. "Going from zero to one is where we get the most bang for our buck," he says. "But if you want to have the most meaningful life, one where you feel bonded and connected to others, more friends are better." [1]

Many studies back this up, including one conducted by Suzanne Degges-White (2020 study), chair of the Counseling and Higher Education Department at Northern Illinois University. She found that women in their late thirties to late sixties who had three or more close friends had higher levels of overall life satisfaction than those who didn't. And if you want to make a lasting impact, having close friends and supportive people in your life is going to make your progress easier and more enjoyable.[2]

"No matter what you decide to do, you'll be better off with your village behind you," I told Melody after I shared this research with her. "I want you to revive your long-distance connections and make some new ones. In the meantime, I can help you gain clarity about what's best for you and your daughters."

It's easy to let relationships slip when we're busy or overwhelmed with life's challenges, but that's when we need to keep our connections the strongest. If we stop investing in those primary relationships, we create barriers to our own happiness and success. In Melody's case, in just two years her marriage slid from happy to barely tolerable, and since she hadn't made new friends, she felt completely alone. Without strong relationships, life is harder and closing the gap between where you are now and where you want to be is an uphill battle.

After I explained this to Melody, she agreed to connect with her old friends more often and join an online network to meet new people and hopefully make some new friends. "Honestly, I've been so wrapped up with the kids and so upset with Peter that I didn't realize how alone I've been feeling," she said.

I also encouraged her to strengthen her relationship with Peter. Since they'd been happily married for years, I didn't want her to give up on rescuing that connection. Their life's layout had changed, and since it was working for Peter, he didn't want to acknowledge how unfair he was being, but they still shared many of the same values. Whether they stayed together or not, it would be good for their kids and good for her to remodel their relationship.

Most relationships can be strengthened in at least a few ways. And because relationships play the biggest role in whether we succeed in making a lasting impact, we need to get better at getting along with each other. As James Clear, author of *Atomic Habits*, says, "The greatest rewards in life are often delayed . . . Meaningful outcomes take a long time to grow and compound . . . If you want your results to continue to grow, then you need relationships that last . . . Many relationships disintegrate before the rewards accumulate."

WHAT MAKES A RELATIONSHIP GOOD?

Just like we all have our own ideas about what it means to make a lasting impact, we all define "good" relationships differently. But however you define them, if you have a strong village, the relationships you spend the most time in should live up to the six relationship standards.

The Six Relationship Standards

Typically, good relationships have the following qualities:

1. **Authenticity:** You feel comfortable being the true version of yourself with the other person.
2. **Encouragement:** They encourage you to grow and evolve.
3. **Safe Space:** They hold a space where you feel safe to dream and envision new opportunities and share your secrets and concerns.
4. **Positive Influence:** They're inspiring and stimulating.
5. **Care and Compassion:** They show concern about your happiness and well-being.
6. **High Expectations:** They hold you to a high standard.

For example, Daniela grew by leaps and bounds when her team leaders were inspiring, welcomed authenticity, created a safe space for her to grow and develop, truly cared about her well-being and happiness, and held her to a high standard. Today at Heineken, the teams she creates and leads all exemplify the six relationship standards, and they're also characterized by assets like respect, honesty, independence, open communication, accountability and, of course, teamwork. She wants her team members to enjoy their jobs as much as she enjoys hers.

"I love developing strong teams and talents, and one of the reasons the teams are strong is because there's no hierarchy in our process," she says. "I talk to the CEO the same way that I talk to my trainee. They both deserve respect, time, and consideration."

Daniela empowers her teams to be autonomous, meaning they can do their jobs how they want and where they want as long as they deliver high-quality work and meet their deadlines. She also wants each individual to be recognized for his or her accomplishments, so like her supervisors Ana Maria and Patricia did, she credits them for their accomplishments. "It's important to acknowledge their achievements and make sure they get credit for them because that will help them to be promoted and also because it creates a strong culture of talent recognition that's good for the company," she says. "With this dynamic we're always working together to become better individually and together, and this is the dynamic in my marriage too."

She smiles as she tells me her husband, Ronaldo (who you met in Chapter One), has always been a positive influence on her. "He has endless optimism and believes every problem has a solution—we just have to find it. Sometimes when I have a problem to solve, I catch myself thinking, *How would Ronaldo solve this?*" She describes her husband as happy and pleasant and admires him because he can get along with everyone. "These are traits I try to emulate," she says. Meanwhile, Ronaldo describes Daniela as the glue that holds their family together. "I wouldn't have been able to achieve my career goals and have such a close family if it wasn't for Dani," he says.

They had to adapt to many different circumstances and scenarios over the years and were able to make the adjustments because they consistently invested in their marriage and in their relationships with friends, family, and colleagues.

"Ronaldo's the best partner I could ask for," Daniela says. "He's been here by my side for twenty-five years, always supporting my choices, even when that meant living in the United States for a year while he was in Brazil."

Daniela and Ronaldo's story is a beautiful example of what two people can create. In addition to investing in and reaping the rewards of a happy marriage, they're both leading meaningful lives and helping to make the world better with collaboration and teamwork. When two people have a close connection, one plus one equals more than two. It's like earning interest. Whatever they can accomplish individually is maximized when they're together. This synergy is a catalyst for potential, so both people grow, accomplish more and become better.

Sometimes the math is easy. When it's on the plus side, you know the relationship is making you a better person. You can see that you're growing. But when you sum up a relationship and get less than two, it's diminishing one or both people. Instead of encouraging growth, it clips your wings. That's what led Rafael to make an appointment with me. After being in an exclusive relationship for almost a year, he said, "I feel trapped. I'm not the same guy I was a year ago and I don't know how to fix this."

He told me his girlfriend, Anelisa, was jealous and insecure because previous boyfriends had cheated on her. "I've never cheated and I've never given her a reason to think I might," he said. "But she's constantly accusing me of wanting to be with other women."

Anelisa didn't like any of Rafael's friends, and the list of people she forbade him to see was growing. Before long, her jealousy extended to his co-workers, and when Rafael's boss said she was taking the whole department to San Diego to celebrate the year they were having, Anelisa said she'd break up with him if he went.

"That's where I should have drawn the line." He ran his fingers through his hair. "I knew it would look bad if I didn't go, but I didn't want to poke the bear."

At his next performance review, his boss told him that skipping the celebration trip was an indication that he wasn't "all in" like the other people in the department and he was passed up for a promotion. His relationship with Anelisa had already lowered his quality of life, but not being promoted showed him that it was also a major detriment to his career. He wanted to rise to an executive level, but with Anelisa, none of that was going to happen.

"If one of your friends told you what you just told me, what would you say?" I asked him.

"Get the hell out."

If he'd have been in my office instead of on my screen, I'd have high-fived him.

Until Rafael learned about the six relationship standards, he didn't know he was in a dysfunctional dynamic. He just knew he was moving further away from where he wanted to be heading. When we see someone in this dynamic, the imbalance is obvious, but when someone is in the midst of chaos, it's hard to have perspective. It's like trying to see the landscape around us from the eye of a hurricane. As Rafael became disconnected from his other relationships, the lines between healthy and unacceptable began to blur. As he lost perspective, the effects of the loss rippled across every part of his life.

Fortunately, the ripple effect can be just as powerful in healthy, helpful ways. When a relationship has most or all of the six standards, it benefits the people involved and has a positive influence on everyone around them. The people in these relationships are our most reliable and consistent council members. They're there for us, they believe in us, and they help us to pursue our purpose.

In *The Prophet*, Kahlil Gibran says:

> *"Your friend is your needs answered.*
> *He is your field which you sow with love*
> *and reap with thanksgiving.*
> *And he is your board and your fireside.*
> *For you come to him with your hunger,*
> *and you seek him for peace."*

Gibran wasn't a psychologist and didn't consider himself a philosopher, but his description of friendship is the most beautiful and accurate that I've read. Good friends not only hold us to high standards, cheer us on and offer refuge from the storms, but they're also good for our health. People with strong relationships have a reduced risk of high blood pressure, depression and obesity, and live longer than those who don't. And because good relationships enhance your sense of belonging and purpose, they magnify your happiness, reduce stress, improve confidence and self-worth and even encourage you to adopt or maintain healthy lifestyle habits. And that can all help you achieve your goals. It's amazing how much friends can influence the way our lives play out. Imagine what your life would be like if your most supportive and generous friends weren't part of it. And now imagine what your life could be like if all of your close relationships were as strong as the most supportive and generous ones. That's how high we should all be aiming.

RELATIONSHIP ASSETS AND LIABILITIES

In addition to the six relationship standards (authenticity, encouragement, safe space, positive influence, care and compassion, and high expectations) good relationships have the following assets:

Relationship Assets

1. **Equality:** Gender, race, age, financial status and education level don't play a role in the relationship. You're on equal footing, and neither person feels superior.

2. **Respect and Admiration:** Mutual respect and admiration are the basis for good relationships. You don't have to always agree, but when you respect your friend's opinion and are able to admire their positive traits, unique characteristics and what they stand for, that's gold.

3. **Honesty and Trust:** Being honest about your feelings or about your intentions goes a long way in building good relationships. Honesty here encompasses truth and transparency. Trust is knowing that what you share won't be judged or shared with others.

4. **Open Communication:** You feel safe telling your friend or partner when you're upset about problems or your relationship and talking about ways to improve things.

5. **Independence and Individuality:** You're separate people. There are hobbies, interests, and friends you share and others you don't. You have your life, they have theirs, and where your lives intersect you

have overlap. Spending time together is important to strengthening the relationship, and spending time apart is important to keeping you both interesting. This is the opposite of codependence, which happens when you rely 100 percent on your friend or partner for emotional or psychological support.

6. **Lightheartedness:** You don't take life too seriously. You're playful and poke fun at yourself and each other. You have inside jokes.

7. **Teamwork:** You work and play well together. You're kind to each other and cheer each other on. You give each other the benefit of the doubt, don't need to walk on eggshells, and know where you stand.

8. **Accountability:** Sometimes we mess up. When that happens, we take responsibility and rely on honesty and open communication to talk through it.

Relationship Liabilities

1. **Dishonesty:** Lying, keeping secrets, being disingenuous, and being unfaithful are toxic to all relationships.

2. **Jealousy:** Needing permission to make plans or spend time with family members or other friends that will eventually damage relationships.

3. **Disrespect:** Disrespectful behaviors include belittling, insulting and making fun of you, your family, or friends. People can also disrespect boundaries—for example, by criticizing religious observances or political views.

4. **Dependence/Codependence:** When you need to be needed and you're in a relationship with someone

who needs you, the dynamic makes you the giver and the other person the taker. Or vice versa. This is not a healthy dynamic and should be avoided.

5. **Harassment or Violence:** Harassment and violence take many forms, but a common effect is being afraid to speak your mind or do what you want because you may suffer physical or psychological consequences.

6. **Diminished Sense of Self:** Being on the receiving end of dishonesty, jealousy, disrespect, dependence and harassment, or violence can all make you feel like you're losing yourself. Over time, these damaging behaviors stunt growth, harm health and make you feel like a bad person or like less of a person.

Exercise: Review Your Relationship Roster

Most people know what's working in their relationships and what's not, but when my clients do a thorough assessment, some of the new information is surprising. Sometimes they see repeating issues showing up in their relationships. Sometimes they think they have a stronger village than they actually do. Reviewing their relationship roster gives them clarity about their current situation. The beauty of this exercise is that even if the initial results aren't what you hoped for, the assets and liabilities list shows you exactly what can be improved.

I encourage you to set aside some time to put serious thought into this exercise because we'll be revisiting it throughout the book:

1. Make a list of the three to five people you spend the most time with. It might include friends, family members, co-workers, neighbors or anyone else who's around a lot.

2. Now, make a list of the three to five other people (not on your first list) who have the most influence over you. They might include one or both parents, siblings, a mentor and even people who influence you even if you wish they didn't. (The people on both lists influence your thoughts and behaviors.)

3. Fill out the table on the next page for each person. Circle the columns according to the instructions.

	Rate Relationship (your subjective rating)	Assets	Liabilities
	How would you describe this relationship at the moment? This has to do with your subjective feeling. Circle appropriate choice	From these relationship assets, circle all or any that are present in this relationship:	From these relationship liabilities, circle all or any that are present in this relationship:
Person 1	1. Awful 2. Needs Improvement 3. Average 4. Good 5. Excellent	1. Equality 2. Respect and Admiration 3. Honesty and Trust 4. Open Communication 5. Independence and Individuality 6. Lightheartedness 7. Teamwork 8. Accountability	1. Dishonesty 2. Jealousy 3. Disrespect 4. Dependence 5. Harassment or Violence 6. Diminished Sense of Self
People 2-10	1. Awful 2. Needs Improvement 3. Average 4. Good 5. Excellent	1. Equality 2. Respect and Admiration 3. Honesty and Trust 4. Open Communication 5. Independence and Individuality 6. Lightheartedness 7. Teamwork 8. Accountability	1. Dishonesty 2. Jealousy 3. Disrespect 4. Dependence 5. Harassment or Violence 6. Diminished Sense of Self

How to Interpret Your Results

When you're assessing your relationships, consider which ones are most aligned with your values and purpose. If you only have two or three people you can count on, find ways to expand your village. Nobody has pinpointed the ideal number of close relationships we should have, but we know that having only one person in our corner may be insufficient and a dozen or more may be too many.

Relationship Assets

If you've circled all or most of the assets for someone on one of your lists, don't be complacent. Work to improve and strengthen what's already working.

If there are assets missing in a particular relationship, take a moment to think about why they might be missing and how they can be developed.

Relationship Liabilities

A relationship with more than one liability can diminish the quality of life for both people. Such relationships require your urgent attention. (See the action guide at the end of the book for steps that can repair relationships.)

YOU CAN STRENGTHEN YOUR VILLAGE

What if there's a significant relationship in your life that doesn't have any of the liabilities but when you interact with this person, you feel awful?

Or what if you have a relationship that has several of the assets but you had a major disagreement or one of you disappointed the other with your actions or words?

In cases like these, consider the relationship's assets and see if they outweigh the liabilities or disappointment. If the person is aligned with your life goals and purpose and you want them to be members of your village, you need to take the steps to improve the relationship. If you don't do anything differently, nothing will change.

What You Can Do

- **Share how you're feeling.** If the relationship doesn't have liabilities but interacting with the person has a negative effect, try to identify why you feel awful when you interact with them. Is it the way they treat you, a certain behavior like interrupting, or a particular attitude that's triggering for you? Once you identify why the interaction is unpleasant, consider sharing how you're feeling—without pointing the finger or attacking the person. Your objective is simply to share how you feel and ask for input. For example, my client Bob values family and loves spending time with his brothers. His relationships with them have all the assets and none of the liabilities. But over the past year or so, he's noticed that his brothers sometimes take little jabs at him—something that didn't used to happen. I suggested that Bob point it out the next time it happened and pay attention to the input they gave him. It turned out that Bob's brothers were a little annoyed with him because he frequently suggested restaurants, concerts, sporting events and other activities that they couldn't easily afford. He hadn't noticed that the jabs were always related to these types of suggestions, but once his brothers told him how they felt, they were all able to laugh about how clueless Bob was about how much things cost. With his new awareness, Bob made more appropriate suggestions and the problem was fixed. If he hadn't asked for input about their jabs, he might still be in the dark and he'd have missed the opportunity to become better.

- **Agree to disagree on the contentious issue or find a way to understand each other's stance without agreeing.** For example, when the COVID-19 vaccines became available, many friends and even family members ended relationships that were otherwise solid, because they disagreed about the safety and effectiveness of the vaccines. When we take a stance, we set ourselves up for resistance in one form or another and can alienate people who are important to us and add meaning to our lives. Instead of letting a single issue or isolated disagreement become a permanent barrier or criticizing someone for their opinion or preference, why not agree to disagree? Learning to respect other people's opinions, especially when they're different from our own, is an important trait of good relationships.

- **Forgive and repair the relationship or re-create it.** Nobody is on their best behavior 100 percent of the time, so when someone does something that disappoints or hurts you, it's helpful to consider the entire history of the relationship before making any rash decisions about cutting ties or retaliating in some way. If you're completely honest with yourself, you might be able to see that the mistake the person made is one that you've made yourself or one that you *could* make in similar circumstances.

Another thing that's helpful about reviewing the history of the relationship is that if what the person said or did isn't congruent with past behavior, it can prevent you from taking it personally. Instead, you can find out if they need some type of help or support. You have a variety of options in these situations, but one that I don't recommend is deciding that an isolated incident is grounds for ending an otherwise strong relationship. I often hear clients in this situation say that the person finally showed their true colors, and I always question that assumption. If that's true, was the person faking being a good friend for all those years?

When someone makes a mistake or hurts you in a way that they haven't hurt you before, they aren't showing their true colors. They're showing their humanity. Resist the emotional knee-jerk to punish a friend for wronging you, because you may end up hurting yourself by denying the relationship the chance to heal or transform. If the relationship was strong before the event, it's probably worth giving the person a second chance.

Building and strengthening your village is one the most important things you can do to narrow the gap between where you are now and where you aim to be.

Purpose + Village = Lasting Impact

But to have a strong village, we need to be able to form and maintain close connections, and we can't do that if we don't appreciate individuality in ourselves and others, have reasonable expectations and learn how to repair relationship injuries. We're all unique, so learning to appreciate each other's individuality is the most important skill we can develop. Having reasonable expectations is essential, including expecting to sometimes be annoyed, angry, disappointed, sad, or hurt by other people, because it's bound to happen, especially in long-term relationships. If you understand this, it won't be such a big deal when it happens.

In every relationship there will be times when we disagree, disappoint, and disapprove.

Our deepest, most meaningful relationships have a variety of positive and negative ingredients, including investment, love, effort, hurt, disappointment, joy, surprise, loyalty, selfishness, and generosity. Since no relationship is turbulence-free, we need to learn how to repair the damage that will inevitably be done. People who don't learn how to make repairs can't maintain relationships. And if you can't maintain the relationships you have, you'll probably spend a lot of time and energy making new friends, dating, and looking for new jobs—time you could be spending working toward your idea of success.

The secrets to relationship success are knowing that hurtful incidents occur in all relationships and becoming proficient with repairs. Ruptures are painful, but they're also opportunities for growth. Mastering the art of repair will strengthen your relationships and help them to grow and evolve. The deeper and more meaningful your relationships become, the richer and more rewarding they'll be and the more they'll help you to make a lasting impact.

———————

IN BRIEF

- Associating with people who make you better is like playing a game or sport with a better player—it raises your own game.
- People you spend time with influence what you talk about, how you behave and even what you value.
- Just like people in your past shaped who you are today, the company you're keeping today is influencing who you'll be tomorrow.
- Develop and strengthen relationships with people who expect a lot from themselves and will expect a lot from you.
- Couples can pursue individual purposes and still have a close connection.
- Strengthening your village is one of the most important things you can do to narrow the gap between where you are now and where you aim to be.
- To have a strong village, we need to be able to form and maintain close connections, and we can't do that if we don't appreciate individuality in ourselves and others, have reasonable expectations, and learn how to repair relationship injuries.
- Since no relationship is turbulence-free, we need to learn how to repair the damage that will inevitably

be done. People who don't learn how to make repairs can't maintain relationships.

The Six Relationship Standards

1. Authenticity
2. Encouragement
3. Safe Space
4. Positive Influence
5. Care and Compassion
6. High Expectations

Relationship Assets

1. Equality
2. Respect and Admiration
3. Honesty and Trust
4. Open Communication
5. Independence and Individuality
6. Lightheartedness
7. Teamwork
8. Accountability

Relationship Liabilities

1. Dishonesty
2. Jealousy
3. Disrespect
4. Dependence/Codependence
5. Harassment or Violence
6. Diminished Sense of Self

———————

In Chapter Four, you'll have a chance to assess your own relationship game and learn how to improve your performance.

CHAPTER 4

RATE YOUR OWN GAME

A long list of former associates knew Celeste was her own worst enemy. A brilliant architect, she could spot a design error in seconds flat, but when it came to seeing how she was destroying her relationships, she was blind. She scheduled an appointment with me because she didn't get the last two promotions she'd applied for and her career had plateaued.

As it turned out, Celeste had experienced the same pattern at previous companies where she worked. Every time she joined a new company, she quickly became a star employee—respected, well-liked and included in everything that was happening inside the office and out. But after six months to a year, the honeymoon would come to a screeching halt as Celeste annihilated one team member after another. Sometimes it was for making a mistake or missing a deadline, and sometimes it was because the team members disagreed with her verdict that she was right and they were wrong.

"It's so unfair," Celeste said when I met with her. "Between the office politics and my slacker team members, I've been passed over for two promotions this year." The possibility that she was the common denominator in all her relationship woes hadn't occurred to her. Sometimes the elephant in the room is so big that it seems to belong there. So the first step was to help her see the role she was playing and encourage her to think about what really mattered to her. Did she like being a lone wolf at work? Or was she happier when her co-workers respected her and included her? Had she considered that the issues she was having with her team might be costing her promotions?

People who successfully climb the corporate ladder have more than just great technical capabilities. They also have strong leadership skills and work well with others. So strengthening relationship skills was a good option for Celeste. Because the quality of our relationships can either help or hinder our ability to succeed, Celeste needed to increase her awareness of how she was showing up in relationships and observe the effect she was having on others. So we began our work together by looking at whether she was adding value to her own village.

ARE YOU ADDING VALUE?

When Celeste listed the qualities she considered imperative in a valuable team member, she realized she couldn't check all the boxes for herself. Yes, she was conscientious about meeting deadlines, did impeccable work and was willing to put in extra hours for the good of the cause, but her communication skills weren't great, especially when she was anxious, and she was stifling her team's creativity with her need to be "right." "I admit I have some improvements to make," she said, "but if everyone else would just do their jobs the way they should be done, I wouldn't get upset with them."

Let's face it—most of us are better at noticing other people's flaws than our own. We view others very differently from how we view ourselves. For one thing, when we interact with someone, we can see their facial expressions but not our own. For another, we notice when someone changes their tone of voice but may not always notice when we do it ourselves. If we want to know how we're doing with our half of a relationship, we need to pay close attention to our thoughts, reactions, and judgments. And we also need to pay close attention to how people respond and react to us. In most cases, the way people feel when we interact with them makes a bigger impression than anything we say or do. We can increase the likelihood that they feel good about an interaction by noticing how they respond and using that input to adjust our own behavior.

When Celeste's team distanced themselves from her, she immediately blamed them instead of considering what she might have done to cause the change in their behavior. It wasn't until I told her she was 50 percent of every relationship that the light bulb turned on. "I never thought of it like that," she said after a long pause. Accepting that she was half the equation helped her see that her attitude and behavior had a huge impact on how other people behaved. When she objectively looked at how she was perpetuating the cycle of being a rising star only to come crashing down, it all became clear.

In the beginning of her new work relationships, Celeste raised the bar for the whole team. She inspired them to reach their goals, generously shared resources and taught them new skills. "I'm so excited when I join a new team," she said. "I like collaborating and coming up with innovative ideas." But at some point she'd begin criticizing instead of encouraging. She had zero tolerance for people who missed deadlines even when sliding the timeline a few days wasn't a real problem, and she didn't make allowances for people getting sick or needing to help a family member. The people who used to feel encouraged and motivated by her now avoided her. Instead of being the project architect who lifted everyone up, she'd turned into the wrecking ball that everyone dived under their desks to avoid.

For Celeste to rise to a senior architect position, she had to come to terms with the fact that she was half of every relationship, and the same is true for all of us. We know good relationships help us succeed, but when a relationship isn't going well, it can be easier to blame the other person than to question whether you're putting in your fair share. Assessing your own relationship skills and making self-improvements will help ensure that people want to be part of your village and want you to be part of theirs.

Exercise: Review the Effect You're Having

In Chapter Three, you looked at the types of qualities you want the people in your village to display. Now we're turning the question around so you can look at whether you're someone who other people want to include in their village.

To get a sense of how you affect others, consider the following questions:

- Do the people I associate with become better? In general, do I add value to other people's lives?
- Do I elevate and inspire people to improve and reach their goals?

- Am I someone people can count on? Do I help friends move, give them doctor referrals or helpful information about restaurants and travel destinations, and have their back when they get sick?
- Am I pleasant and cooperative?

You can also consider feedback you've received from your friends and co-workers:

- Do I like the words they use to describe me?
- Do I get invited to parties and other social events?
- Do people ask me for help?
- Do people confide in me, share their secrets and concerns and ask for advice?

If your answer to most of these questions on both lists is yes, you probably have good relationship skills.

———————

Another way to evaluate your relationship skills is with your internal compass. Sometimes you just know you did good. Maybe it was when you were pressed for time but managed to be patient and kind or when someone admitted you were right and you didn't say, "I told you so." Or maybe it's because you went out of your way to mentor or offer encouragement to someone who was questioning their ability to succeed. In those types of situations, you don't need anyone to affirm that you made a good choice or did something good—you know you're shining.

But there are also times when you're not so radiant. While

nobody's proud of their lackluster moments, when we look at them objectively, they offer us clues about how we can improve our interactions. Being more self-reflective about the value you bring to relationships and committing to improving your skills will help you to leave the legacy you want to leave. But for the assessment to be useful, you have to be honest and critical, and most people need some practice at this. As Stephen R. Covey, author of *The 7 Habits of Highly Effective People,* says, "We judge ourselves by our intentions and others by their behavior." Imagine how much we could improve our relationships if we judged others by their intentions and judged *ourselves* by our behavior.

I'm inviting you to be more objective about yourself than you've ever been. Your mission is to figure out how you can improve your relationship skills and set measurable goals for continued growth and improvement. We all know that getting better at something takes practice, but people often think that relationships can or should take care of themselves. This couldn't be further from the truth. Strong relationships require strong relationship skills. Strengthening these skills will help you to become the person you want to be and to make a lasting impact that's meaningful to you.

Exercise: Assess Your Performance

This is an opportunity to practice being objectively critical of yourself. When one plus one equals less than two in a relationship, it's your responsibility to figure out how you're contributing to the deficit. If you don't implicate yourself in some way, you're being too generous with yourself and passing up the chance to grow.

For this exercise, you'll use the same list of assets and liabilities you used to rate the health of your relationships in Chapter Three. Only this time, you'll be evaluating your own relationship performance.

Assets	Liabilities
1. Equality	1. Dishonesty
2. Respect and Admiration	2. Jealousy
3. Honesty and Trust	3. Disrespect
4. Open Communication	4. Dependence
5. Independence and Individuality	5. Harassment or Violence
6. Lightheartedness	6. Diminished Sense of Self
7. Teamwork	
8. Accountability	

Answer the following questions, using the list above:

1. Review the assets in the chart and list the ones you always or almost always bring to your relationships.
2. List the assets that are the most challenging for you. These will show you opportunities for growth.
3. Review the liabilities in the chart and list the ones you sometimes bring to a relationship.

Refer to the Review Your Relationship Roster exercise you did in Chapter Three and answer the following questions. Your goal is to implicate yourself in as many ways as possible, keeping in mind that you're half of every relationship.

1. For the relationships that have missing items in the asset column, how might your behavior be contributing to this?
2. For the relationships that have one or more items in the liability column, how might your behavior be contributing to this?

Once you identify areas for your own improvement, you can create a plan to grow the assets that are challenging for you and strengthen the skills to eliminate the liabilities you bring to relationships.

Seeing how your behaviors may be contributing to the issues that are barriers to your success can motivate you to make improvements, and even small improvements add up to big impacts.

VALUES MOTIVATE BEHAVIOR

When Celeste looked at her relationships at work more objectively, she realized that she was causing a lot of the problems but wasn't ready to accept that it was her responsibility to fix them. "I care more about how the team does than everybody else put together," she said. "Why am I the one who has to change? It's their job to work hard so we can all get promotions. But it's one distraction after another with them."

The "distractions" Celeste complained about included taking care of ill family members, celebrating birthdays, attending their kids' sporting events and family vacations—all reflections of what her co-workers valued in life. Family and fun were as important to them as career success and productivity were to Celeste. "I know their families are important, but at work I think they should put their professional reputations first like I do," she said.

"Values are very personal," I said. "They're unique to each person, and no value is better than another. The reason it's helpful to know your values is because whatever you consider essential or extremely important motivates how you behave and the choices you make. Knowing your values helps you to know what's good and worthwhile for you, but if you judge other people according to your values, they'll always come up short. It's not a fair assessment."

She nodded, but I didn't get the sense that she was totally on board, so I explained that we all have different values because our values are formed by our individual life stories. "Values are formed by our innate qualities, upbringing, culture and the influence our villages had on us. But that doesn't mean they're carved into stone. As we gain knowledge and life experience, sometimes we reconsider our values and might even change them."

"You mean like how I used to devour meat and now I'm a vegetarian and belong to PETA [People for the Ethical Treatment of Animals]?" Celeste asked.

"That's a great example," I said, "but even though values can change, they're uniquely personal because they stem from our individual stories. That's why it's easier to understand people when we know and respect their values. And when we know our own values, it helps us to understand our motivations."

"That makes sense," Celeste said, "but I still think everyone on a project team should value becoming more successful."

"What if someone's striving to build an incredible family or has a deep belief in maintaining a balance between work and life?" I said.

She shook her head. "Shouldn't they focus on becoming financially stable and grow in their career *first*?"

"That may be the road for you," I said, "but what if they don't value that as much as you do? Maybe it's more important to them to spend time with their family or they just want to enjoy life while they're young. Those people may prefer a slower route to financial independence. Or maybe financial independence isn't even a goal for them. Are their values wrong or just different?"

She laughed. "I know the right answer is 'They're just different,' but they still seem wrong to me. I guess I should do that assessment you suggested."

Identifying your core values is a prerequisite for self-improvement because you can only improve what you know and understand. When you see that what's most valuable to you is personal and unique, you can extend that awareness to others and become more open-minded. With this type of awareness, you understand that people's decisions and actions, like your own, are motivated by unique core values.

Exercise: Identify Your Core Values

If you know what your core values are, this exercise can give you even more clarity. If you haven't identified your values, there's no time like the present.

1. Review the following list of values,[1] and if you have values that aren't on this list, add them:

- Acceptance: to be accepted as I am
- Accuracy: to be accurate in my opinions and beliefs
- Achievement: to have important accomplishments
- Adventure: to have new and exciting experiences
- Attractiveness: to be physically attractive
- Authority: to be in charge of and responsible for others
- Autonomy: to be self-determined and independent
- Beauty: to appreciate beauty around me
- Caring: to take care of others
- Challenge: to take on difficult tasks and problems
- Change: to have a life full of change and variety
- Comfort: to have a pleasant and comfortable life
- Commitment: to make enduring, meaningful commitments
- Compassion: to feel and act on concern for others
- Contribution: to make a lasting contribution in the world
- Cooperation: to work collaboratively with others
- Courtesy: to be considerate and polite toward others
- Creativity: to have new and original ideas
- Dependability: to be reliable and trustworthy
- Duty: to carry out my duties and obligations
- Ecology: to live in harmony with the environment
- Excitement: to have a life full of thrills and stimulation
- Faithfulness: to be loyal and true in relationships
- Fame: to be known and recognized
- Family: to have a happy, loving family
- Fitness: to be physically fit and strong
- Flexibility: to adjust to new circumstances easily

- Forgiveness: to be forgiving of others
- Friendship: to have close, supportive friends
- Fun: to play and have fun
- Generosity: to give what I have to others
- Genuineness: to act in a manner that is true to who I am
- God's Will: to seek and obey the will of God
- Growth: to keep changing and growing
- Health: to be physically well and healthy
- Helpfulness: to be helpful to others
- Honesty: to be honest and truthful
- Hope: to maintain a positive and optimistic outlook
- Humility: to be modest and unassuming
- Humor: to see the humorous side of myself and the world
- Independence: to be free from dependence on others
- Industry: to work hard and well at my life tasks
- Inner peace: to experience personal peace
- Intimacy: to share my innermost experiences with others
- Justice: to promote fair and equal treatment for all
- Knowledge: to learn and contribute valuable knowledge
- Leisure: to take time to relax and enjoy
- Loved: to be loved by those close to me
- Loving: to give love to others
- Mastery: to be competent in my everyday activities
- Mindfulness: to live conscious and mindful of the present moment
- Moderation: to avoid excesses and find a middle ground
- Monogamy: to have one close, loving relationship

- Nonconformity: to question and challenge authority and norms
- Nurturance: to take care of and nurture others
- Openness: to be open to new experiences, ideas and options
- Order: to have a life that is well-ordered and organized
- Passion: to have deep feelings about ideas, activities and people
- Pleasure: to feel good
- Popularity: to be well-liked by many people
- Power: to have control over others
- Purpose: to have meaning and direction in my life
- Rationality: to be guided by reason and logic
- Realism: to see and act realistically and practically
- Responsibility: to make and carry out responsible decisions
- Risk: to take risks and chances
- Romance: to have intense, exciting love in my life
- Safety: to be safe and secure
- Self-Acceptance: to accept myself as I am
- Self-Control: to be disciplined in my own actions
- Self-Esteem: to feel good about myself
- Self-Knowledge: to have a deep and honest understanding of myself
- Service: to be of service to others
- Sexuality: to have an active and satisfying sex life
- Simplicity: to live life simply, with minimal needs
- Solitude: to have time and space where I can be apart from others
- Spirituality: to grow and mature spiritually
- Stability: to have a life that stays fairly consistent

- Tolerance: to accept and respect those who differ from me
- Tradition: to follow respected patterns of the past
- Virtue: to live a morally pure and excellent life
- Wealth: to have plenty of money
- World Peace: to work to promote peace in the world

2. Place the values above, including those you may have added, into three categories:

- Very important to me
- Important to me
- Not important to me.

Try to make these decisions without thinking about expectations that other people or society may have of you. Also keep in mind that no value is intrinsically more valuable than the others. Your highest values are someone else's lowest, and vice versa. Values are very personal, so do your best to keep judgment out of this process.

3. From the Very Important category, choose the five values that are the *most* important to you.

As you review your past, you'll probably notice that the good decisions you made were aligned with your very important core values and that the choices you regret are not. With clarity about these values, you can intentionally keep them front and center and make sure your decisions and actions are aligned with them. These principles are all about what you value most. They shouldn't reflect anyone else's expectations.

4. Rank the five most important values, with #1 being the most important.

Not everyone can clearly rank the top five values, so if you're having trouble, consider what your list might look like if you *had* to rank them? When you think about how to prioritize your values, keep in mind that your most important values motivate your actions. They serve as a moral compass that points at whatever is essential or important to you. As you're selecting your top values, keep in mind that no value is intrinsically more valuable than the others.

If you find this exercise challenging, you don't need to finish it in one day. Give yourself the gift of reflection, sleep on it and try to finish it the following day. Remember, there are no right answers, and maybe you'll have a "tie" in the ranking. The purpose of the exercise is to increase self-awareness, so if the exercise is getting you to think, it's achieving its goal.

Celeste was a serial self-saboteur because she believed that her core values—achievement, challenge, and industry—were "right," not just for her, but for everyone. But when she evaluated her behavior based on her team members' values, she was the one who appeared to come up short. That realization, along with her new awareness that improving her relationships would advance her career, convinced her that she needed to make some improvements. She began to practice seeing situations through the lens of her team members' values and considering their perspectives. This wasn't easy for

Celeste and she still struggles with it, but now that she knows strengthening her relationships is essential to her own success, she's willing to do what it takes.

Knowing the hierarchy of your values helps you to make difficult decisions because you're clear about what's most important to you. Let's say your company offers your department a fabulous opportunity that will advance your career and comes with a salary increase, but if you accept the job, you'll need to move to another city or state. If your highest core values are autonomy, commitment and family, you may take the job because growing in your career is aligned with having more autonomy. Because you value commitment, you may be motivated to stick with your departmental team and your company, and if you were involved in the new venture's inception, you want to see it through. With family as one of your core values, you'll probably want your partner and children to move with you or will visit them often.

If your core values are contribution, duty and friendship, you may not take the job, knowing you can make a meaningful contribution where you are. If duty is a core value, you may feel like it's your responsibility to remain close to your aging parents or your adult children. With friendship as a core value, it may be hard to imagine finding a group of friends like the one you already have. Spending time with your social support network may be worth more to you than any money or professional position.

Both of these examples illustrate how values help us to make choices and demonstrate that what's right for one person can be wrong for another.

EXERCISE YOUR FREEDOM TO CHOOSE

American existential psychiatrist Irvin Yalom says freedom is one of the four existential concerns that humans have, along with death, meaninglessness, and existential isolation. The reason freedom is an existential concern is because if you believe human beings have free will and the ultimate freedom to do what we want, we're 100 percent responsible for the outcomes we create. So, paradoxically, freedom can both give us wings and weigh us down. Freedom is empowering and exciting because it makes us the owner and CEO of our life, but freedom can also be a burden. "To be aware of responsibility is to be aware of creating one's own self, destiny, life predicament, feelings and, if such is the case, one's own suffering,"[2] Yalom says.

Although freedom is a double-edged sword, if you wield it with awareness and clear intention, you can improve yourself, your relationships, and the future. But like anything else, getting good at exercising your freedom takes practice and can be challenging. Accepting your freedom goes hand in hand with making difficult choices, including distancing yourself from relationships that are hindering the future you envision. If there are people in your village who bring out your worst, they're probably not helping you to make the lasting impact you want to make. But observing your reaction to their behavior can help you identify the triggers that set you off, and that's valuable information.

In Chapter Seven, I'll give you tools to help decide if there are relationships you need to distance yourself from. But for now, if there are people in your life who bring out your worst, try treating them the way the best version of you would, regardless of how they behave or whether you think they deserve it. Doing this is one of the most powerful ways you can express your freedom.

Consider this example. Rachel is a successful attorney who's on her way to becoming a partner in a prominent law firm. Her co-workers respect her and she's well-regarded in the legal community, but when she goes home to visit her parents she feels like an insecure teenager again. "They push every one of my buttons," she said. "They wanted me to work in the family business like my brother. When I passed the bar exam, instead of congratulating me, my father said I'd sold myself short." She sighed and shook her head. "I don't know why I'm obsessed with making them proud of me. After all these years, you'd think I'd quit trying."

At the office Rachel was confident and charismatic, but with her parents she was defensive and quick to take offense. Not only did she feel like an insecure teenager, but she behaved like one too. She was cynical and sarcastic and even mocked her mother, which she was particularly ashamed of. "If people at work saw the way I am with my parents, they'd have a hard time believing it was me," she said.

What Rachel didn't realize was that she had the freedom to shift the relationship dynamic no matter how her parents behaved or what they said. Instead of trying to change their behavior, she could change her interpretation and reaction. "If they criticize you," I said, "instead of taking it personally and being defensive, let it go in one ear and out the other. If you want to make it even more interesting, find something amusing about it. When someone cuts my brother off in traffic, he likes to wave and say, 'I forgive you,' or, 'You're welcome!'"

Rachel laughed. "That would be an improvement, for sure."

Because you have the freedom to choose how you behave, if someone annoys you, try doing a gratitude exercise instead of ruminating about their behavior or fantasizing about getting even. Start by thinking of a few things they did that were helpful or kind to you or someone else. Keep thinking of things you can be grateful to them about until you can see that they're making a positive contribution to you, others, or the world. If your mind resists this level of gratitude, consider the ways this person is contributing to your personal growth. Is interacting with them helping you to become a little more patient, resilient, or tolerant?

I recognize that choosing to be grateful to someone who acts like a jerk sounds absurd, but if you change your mindset, you won't be as reactive. That will reduce friction and allow you to focus your thoughts and energy on something productive. If you identify as a kind person, that's what you can be, no matter how the people around you behave. Treating people who have the ability to bring out your worst as well as you treat those who bring out your best is the kind of consistency to strive for. That said, the more people in your village who bring out your best, the faster you can progress toward your definition of success. So use your freedom of choice to intentionally surround yourself with people who bring out your best as often as you can.

Exercise: Who's in Your Village?

Refer to your Relationship Roster in Chapter Three. Think about how you show up in these relationships and answer the following questions:

1. Who brings out the best in me?
2. Who am I most comfortable with and inspired by?
3. Who brings out the worst in me?
4. What do they say or do that triggers me?

———————

My village includes my family and all of my incredibly supportive and inspiring friends. In addition to sharing some of the same values, they're kind, patient, generous, cooperative and courageous. We encourage each other to be better, do better, get more involved in things we want to change and be more consistent with our own progress. When your village has people like these, you'll be consistently motivated to grow and make the changes that lead to a more meaningful life.

My new clients often say, "If only my wife (or husband, parents, kids, co-workers, boss, etc.) would change." I help them to see that by placing the blame on the other person, they're forfeiting their freedom to choose how to respond and how to move forward.

When Rachel realized she had the freedom to focus on the gratitude she had for her parents instead of their criticism, she stopped being defensive. But what she appreciated even more was the realization that she could improve the relationship without changing her parents. "When it sank in that I have the freedom to be who I am and can choose to be grateful for who they are, our whole relationship changed," she said and smiled. "I actually like going home now."

When we're having a problem with a relationship, there are three ways that people usually look at it. One is to believe that the other person is predominantly responsible for the problems. Another is to believe that you are predominantly responsible for the problems. And the third is to believe it takes two people to change a relationship. None of these beliefs are true. We have the freedom and power to improve the quality of our relationships by reframing the problems or conflicts and changing our mindset. The other person doesn't have to change or even know that we're working on the relationship.

Like Celeste and Rachel, we all have the freedom to strengthen our relationships by honoring others' values without compromising our own.

IN BRIEF

- If you want to know how you're doing with your half of a relationship, pay close attention to your thoughts, reactions, and judgments and to how people respond and react to you.
- Assessing your own game and making self-improvements will ensure that people want to be on your team and want you on theirs.
- While nobody's proud of their lackluster moments, when you look at them objectively, they offer you clues about how you can improve your interactions and your relationships.
- Strong relationships require strong relationship skills. Strengthening these skills will help you to close the gap between who you are now and who you want to be.

- Identifying your core values is a prerequisite for self-improvement because you can only improve what you know and understand. When you see that what's most valuable to you is personal and unique, you can extend that awareness to others and become more open-minded. With this type of awareness, you understand that people's decisions and actions, like your own, are motivated by unique core values.
- The reason freedom is an existential concern is because if you believe human beings have free will and the ultimate freedom to do what we want, we're 100 percent responsible for the outcomes we create.
- Freedom is a double-edged sword, but if you wield it with awareness and clear intention, you can improve yourself, your relationships and your future.

In Chapter Five, you'll learn how to upgrade your communication skills.

CHAPTER 5

UPGRADE YOUR COMMUNICATION SKILLS

Bella lived up to her name. It was easy to see how the passionate Italian artist with dark hair and a contagious smile had caught Trevor's eye—and held it. The fairytale romance began with a chance meeting at the Palazzo Ducale museum in Venice, and before he flew back to New York, they'd pledged their love in a gondola on the Canal Grande. A couple of months later, Bella moved in with Trevor—he was an account manager for an advertising agency and couldn't move to Italy, but she could live anywhere. A small wedding followed a short engagement, and two years later they celebrated the birth of their son.

"The first years were unreal," Trevor said. "I felt like the luckiest guy in the world." But soon after Mario was born, the arguments began. "It was like we started talking different languages or something. No matter what I said, she'd turn it into a putdown."

The way Trevor saw it, Bella was the problem. But when I met with her, she said Trevor was questioning everything she did. "Before Mario was born, Trevor was my biggest fan," she said. "He was always complimenting me and telling me how creative I was. But I swear, the day Mario was born, he changed. All of a sudden it was, 'Are you sure you should be using that formula? And isn't it time for his nap?' Last night when I was giving Mario his bath, Trevor came in and had the nerve to say, 'Isn't that water too high?'" She gave me a little smirk. "I've been giving Mario baths for a year now and not a single drowning yet."

If Bella and Trevor were going to save their marriage, they'd both have to take responsibility for their half of the relationship. Even if the other person doesn't make improvements, strengthening our half is an opportunity to practice being our best self. Behaving with poise and grace when we're triggered develops emotional maturity and resilience. Of course, you can choose to dig in your heels and try to get the other person to change, but how often have you seen *that* work?

When Mario turned four, Trevor and Bella were still convinced that their problems would be resolved if only the other person would change. They came back to therapy because their endless arguments were upsetting Mario, and when they appeared on the screen for their appointment, Bella was unusually quiet and Trevor looked like he hadn't slept in days. He explained that he was working long hours on a major ad campaign, Bella was busy getting ready for a new exhibition and Mario had suddenly started having meltdowns when they dropped him off at day care. "He used to like day care," Trevor said. "Now when we pull into the parking lot, he starts crying and says he wants to go to his Nonni's, Bella's mom."

By the end of the session, they'd accepted that they were both at least somewhat responsible for the constant conflict and agreed that they had work to do. I was happy to hear it, but I knew it wouldn't be enough to turn their relationship around. "Insights are a great first step," I said. "They open up possibilities and give us new questions to explore. But insights alone are rarely enough to make lasting changes." They nodded, but I wasn't convinced I'd gotten through.

Allen Wheelis, author of *How People Change*, says, "The most common illusion of patients and, strangely, even of experienced therapists is that insight produces change; and the most common disappointment of therapy is that it does not. Insight is instrumental to change, often an essential part of the process, but does not directly achieve it."

In other words, identifying something you want to change is just the first step. Next you need to make it happen. When you realize you're not fated to act the same way forever, the options to change and improve become available to you. This "aha!" often empowers people to take action to ensure that their new awareness will lead to change. When someone says, "I've always been this way. That's just how I am. I'm too old to change," it can look like they're choosing to stay stuck in place, and maybe they are, but it's also possible that they don't believe they have the freedom to change or don't think they're up for the task. If this is true for you, I encourage you to experiment so you can learn firsthand that you *can* change and grow.

To be worthy of a strong village, capitalize on the knowledge that freedom and responsibility are joined at the hip. If you know you're free to change and you don't make improvements, you're essentially choosing not to bring the best version of yourself to your community and running the risk of losing all the benefits those strong relationships provide. But if you're willing to make improvements, you enhance your chances of making a lasting impact. Hallmarks of healthy relationships include cooperating, negotiating conflict, and offering and asking for help. Whether you're good at these skills often comes down to how well you can actively listen and clearly communicate, because communication skills are a prerequisite for many other relationship skills. This may seem like common sense, but it's not common practice. As playwright George Bernard Shaw said, "The single biggest problem in communication is the illusion that it has taken place."

I shared all this with Trevor and Bella and they understood it intellectually, but the negative images they'd formed of each other had solidified to the point where no matter what one of them said or did, the other took offense. Instead of doing the work to improve the way they communicated, they were acting like squabbling preteens—shouting, slamming doors and calling each other nasty names. It was such a shame because we *can* change—we just have to take action to make it happen.

You've probably noticed that when a relationship is going well, communicating is easy. You understand what the other person is saying, and when you don't, you feel comfortable asking them to explain. But when a relationship is strained or there's a conflict, communicating can be hard because the stakes are higher and the ability to negotiate doesn't come naturally. Since disagreements are a natural part of life, we can all benefit by learning how to navigate them.

When I taught courses to divorcing parents to help minimize the negative impact on their kids, I learned that reasonable people disagree on a reasonable number of things a reasonable amount of time. Whether a disagreement leads to greater understanding or greater conflict depends on how we address it. If we can resolve it, compromise or respectfully agree to disagree, we accrue relationship credit. If not, the disagreement becomes a debit in the relationship's "bank account." If the bank account has a credit balance, the other person is more likely to forgive us when we mess up. When a relationship is "in the red," there's very little leeway. Anything we do or say, no matter how well-intended, can be taken wrong and create conflict. I stress the importance of good communication with all my clients because we can't have strong relationships without it. There's an array of communication skills, but listening closely and expressing yourself clearly form the foundation for all the others.

LISTEN WITH YOUR FULL ATTENTION

It took about a year, but by the time Mario started kindergarten, Trevor and Bella had learned to stop interrupting each other. They hadn't learned to actively listen, though. They were keeping their mouths closed while the other spoke, but they weren't considering what the other one said; they were just waiting to make their own point or counterpoint. It was exhausting. No wonder Mario wanted to go to Nonni's. Thirty minutes into their session, I wanted to go to Nonni's too.

Rubem Alves, a Brazilian theologian, philosopher, educator, writer and psychoanalyst, says being silent while someone is talking isn't really listening if we're thinking about what we want to say or waiting for our turn to talk. He calls it "waiting time," as in "I'm waiting for this person to stop speaking so I can tell them 'the truth' (my point of view)." To truly listen, we have to be humble enough to consider alternative views and "truths."

Instead of waiting for your turn to talk, what if you gave the other person your full attention and listened with curiosity? When we're listening to learn, we ask thoughtful questions and carefully consider the answers. Alves says that if we actively listen and take the other person seriously, we'll be quiet for a while after they finish speaking, giving ourselves a chance to reflect on what they said, especially if it's something that's different or strange to us. When our response is fast or immediate, Alves says, it means, "I don't need to hear you. It's enough to hear myself. I'm not wasting my time dwelling on what you said. What you said isn't what I would have said, so it must be wrong."

Just about every day, a client says something like "It's as if he's not even listening." Or "How many times do I have to tell her this before she gets it?" Or "I'm just wasting my breath." If you were limited to strengthening only one communication skill, becoming a better listener would be your best bet. Tania Israel, psychology professor and author of *Beyond Your Bubble*, says, "If you rearrange the letters of the word *listen*, it spells *silent*." She says that when you interrupt someone while they're talking, "what it's going to do is communicate that you don't actually care very much about what that person is saying and it's going to make them not want to share more with you."

Like Alves, Israel recommends entering a conversation with intellectual humility. When you do this, she says, you're "recognizing that you can still hold your own views and be interested in and respectful of somebody else's."

If someone is talking and you're thinking about why they're wrong, it takes a tremendous amount of effort to remain silent. But if you open your mind to understand their point of view, staying silent is easier, and chances are you'll learn something. With this approach, far from being a chore, silence is intellectually stimulating. Try to see it as the gift that it is. The Active Listener's mantra is, "Mind open, mouth closed."

To be an active listener, practice:

- Giving your full attention to the person who's speaking (yes, that means phone away, not having parallel thoughts in your mind, or zoning out)
- Nodding silently to let them know you're listening
- Paying attention to their words, body language, and facial expressions
- Trying to understand what they're saying from their perspective
- Thinking about what they've said after they finish speaking and asking questions to enhance your understanding

LISTEN TO LEARN

Listening with curiosity gives us the opportunity to learn something and makes conversations more interesting and enjoyable than trying to convince someone that our opinion is the right one. When we approach conversations with this frame of mind, there's nothing to lose and a lot to potentially gain. Curiosity opens our mind and makes us receptive to new ways of thinking. It also makes it possible for us to have strong relationships with people we don't agree with. A fabulous example of this type of relationship was the close friendship between two US Supreme Court justices with opposing views.

Ruth Bader Ginsburg, nicknamed the Notorious RBG, was known for her liberal views, and Antonin Scalia was as conservative as Ginsburg was liberal, but instead of being put off by one another, they enhanced each other's understanding of a wide variety of cases. Their disagreements, which were many, never undermined the integrity of their friendship.

At Scalia's funeral, Ginsburg shared a story about how he helped her to strengthen her argument against his opinion that it was constitutional for the Virginia Military Institute to refuse to accept women. His unfinished dissent "was a zinger," she said, "filled with disdainful footnotes," but instead of being angry or offended, she was grateful because it allowed her to strengthen her argument. "My final draft was much improved thanks to Justice Scalia's searing criticism," she said.

In the almost forty years that they worked together, Scalia and Ginsburg disagreed more than they agreed, but as vehemently as they attacked each other's ideas, they never lashed out at each other personally, and they considered their disagreements par for the course. Imagine how much progress we could make if we stopped polarizing and strived for this type of exchange. When everyone agrees, nobody learns anything. As Brazilian playwright Nelson Rodrigues says, "Unanimity is always stupid!"

Since your opinion or way of doing something is just one of many ways, there's no downside to understanding other opinions and approaches. You can only gain by being curious. When someone disagrees with you, it's an opportunity to review your beliefs. You might learn something that causes you to change your mind, or you might learn something that solidifies your stance. So instead of surrounding yourself only with people who agree with you, better yourself by befriending your own version of Ginsburg or Scalia.

I had the opportunity to learn how powerful curiosity is when I was training to become a psychotherapist and saw a therapist's recorded interview with a man who'd been charged with domestic abuse. My first reaction was, *This guy's a jerk for hitting women. I think I'd have a hard time seeing a client like this.* But the therapist didn't show any negativity toward the man. She was sincerely trying to understand, from his point of view, why he thought it was okay to hit his wife.

She was asking nonthreatening questions about their relationship, and the client, who I'll call A. J., started talking about his wife's going back to college. Soon, it became clear that A. J. was insecure about her need for independence, but at that point I was still annoyed with him. I was thinking he was wrong for believing he had a right to hold his wife back and for hitting her. I wasn't curious. I was judging, which is what people tend to do when we're not curious. When we *are* curious, we ask questions that help us to see the world from someone else's perspective.

The therapist was curious about the "why" behind the abuse, and as she asked one insightful question after another, A. J. began to emerge as a human being. The man I was judging was insecure and scared. He didn't know how to navigate a world where his wife was more educated and knew more than he did. Finally, he said he was worried his wife would meet someone at school who was more educated and interesting than he was and she'd leave him.

This didn't justify his abuse, but the minute I understood his perspective, I stopped seeing him as a jerk and started seeing him as a human being with deep insecurities that had never been addressed. I was starting to understand his "why," and that's essential because it's easier to change behavior when we know what's motivating it. We don't look for underlying causes to justify or rationalize behavior—we look for causes so we can address them. Before he started therapy, A. J. had no idea why he was hitting his wife. When his therapist helped him to understand why he was resorting to violence, A. J. wanted to change his behavior and committed to staying in therapy to learn how. So while insight alone doesn't elicit change, it can lead to the desire for change and encourage us to take action.

A. J. needed to learn how to manage his fear and anger, but for him to be able to do that, he'd first need to improve his self-esteem and become more secure with himself and in his relationship. Understanding the motivation behind a behavior doesn't justify the behavior, but we can't maintain relationships if we jump to judgments instead of learning about the underlying causes.

Understanding the "why" is critically important to maintaining relationships. Why is your co-worker for or against vaccines? Why is your uncle for or against gun control? Why is your neighbor for or against abortion? Try to understand their reasoning. Understanding doesn't mean agreeing. It just means you can see things from their point of view. Understanding their reasoning can help you to form a more educated opinion. It can also help you moderate your own opinions, because when you see something from a variety of perspectives, you're less likely to hold radical views.

COMMUNICATE WITH INTENTION

"When Bella puts her hands on her hips, even the dog takes cover," Trevor said. Meanwhile, Bella was complaining about Trevor's tone: "It's not what he says—it's how he says it."

Words are just one part of communication. Your body language and tone of voice are saying things too, and they can turn your audience on or off, regardless of what you're saying. Whether the audience is your children, your friends or a roomful of strangers, how you come across affects the way your message is heard and received. Putting your hands on your hips, crossing your arms, leaning forward or back and raising or lowering your voice are all forms of communication. If your boss furrows her eyebrows when she says, "Who came up with this?" it might look like she doesn't like the idea. But if she smiles when she asks the question, you know she likes it. If you seem angry or threatening, your audience will feel uncomfortable and possibly defensive. If you smirk when someone comments or asks you a question, it can come across as arrogance. If you're slouching and sighing, people will assume you're tired or bored. Everything you do communicates something, so do yourself a favor by becoming more mindful of what your body and tone are saying.

Researchers have been studying the effects of nonverbal communication since the early 1950s, and one of the most well-known studies was conducted by Albert Mehrabian, professor emeritus of psychology at the University of California Los Angeles (UCLA), in the 1960s. The study found that when we're listening to someone, 55 percent of what we take in is visual, 38 percent is vocal, and only 7 percent is verbal—the actual words they're saying. The study focused on situations where people's words and facial expressions didn't match, and in those cases people usually believed the expressions more than the spoken words. In other words, if you say yes and shake your head, people are likely to assume you mean no.[1]

The study's conclusion became known as the Mehrabian Formula and was later criticized by the scientific community because it didn't prove to be true in all situations and environments. In autocratic environments, for example, people in subordinate positions do what their leader commands, even when the leader's facial expression or body language seems to conflict with their words. But the formula does tend to hold true in democratic environments, especially when the conversation is emotionally charged and there's an intense need to communicate clearly and be understood. Even though Mehrabian's research was criticized for being limited to one aspect of communication, he was a pioneer in demonstrating the dominant role that nonverbal communication plays when we talk about how we're feeling. And today, the consensus among researchers is that over 70 percent of all communication is nonverbal.

Nonverbal Upgrades to Practice

Keep a Nonthreatening Stance and Facial Expression
If you cross your arms in front of your chest, put your hands or fists on your hips, avoid making eye contact, or invade someone's personal space, they'll probably see you as defensive, confrontational, dishonest, or aggressive. If it looks like you're frowning when people are talking to you, they'll interpret your expression as negative or disapproving even if you actually support what they're saying. So-called "resting bitch face" isn't exclusive to females—plenty of men sport perpetual frowns too. And in both cases, they often have no idea that people think they're upset or angry.

If you suspect you have a negative resting-face expression, ask your most honest friend for their opinion. If they confirm your suspicion, make a conscious attempt to keep a slight smile on your face. While conducting research at the University of North Carolina at Chapel Hill, Neil Hester, PhD, found that we infer what others are feeling based on their facial expressions. He says, "Humans automatically form first impressions based on others' appearance, including their perceived emotional state. When others' facial expressions are neutral, or 'resting,' people nevertheless infer emotion."[2]

Having a pleasant resting face so that we're not perceived as unfriendly or unapproachable is so valuable that people are having plastic surgery and other procedures to improve their resting face. But most people can fix this problem themselves by retraining their facial muscles. I'm not suggesting a full-on fake smile, which would be creepy—just check in with your face throughout the day and increase the tension in your lips a tiny bit so they turn upward. I think you'll be amazed by how differently people respond to you.

Center Yourself and Be Still

When you're emotionally centered and physically still, you have a calming influence on the people around you. If you observe others, you'll notice that effective leaders often demonstrate these behaviors and so do effective parents. Fidgeting, tapping your fingers, checking your messages and frequently shifting your position are behaviors associated with being nervous or bored. If this is something you struggle with, consider starting a yoga practice, learning to meditate or increasing your physical activity to burn off the excess energy.

Do a Sound Check

"I'm over these head games," Trevor said. "I asked Bella if she was okay with me going to Atlantic City for a few days and she said, and I quote, 'If that's what you want to do, fine.' Then, when I got home, there was a note on the fridge that said, 'Took Mario to Mom's for a few days,' as if Mom's was across town. What kind of vengeful woman takes her kid to *another country* without telling her husband?"

I'd worked with Trevor and Bella on adjusting their voices to be more respectful to each other, but Bella was having a hard time changing. Being sarcastic and raising her voice were second nature to her, and Trevor couldn't interpret her vocal variations nearly as well as he could read her body language. Learning to hear the variations in someone's voice and controlling the way your own voice sounds are essential communication skills. Your vocal cords work a lot like a stringed instrument, so you can learn to vary your tone, pitch, speed, and volume to match your message. If you're happy about the news you're sharing, you can make sure it comes across in your body language and voice by smiling and speaking with enthusiasm. For some people that might mean talking a little faster, and for others it might mean talking a little louder.

You know what your "happy" sounds like, and you probably know how you sound when you're angry or frustrated. (If you don't, just check with your kids or your partner—*they* know.) But what about all the emotions between happy and angry? How do you speak when you want to show you're interested? What do you sound like when you're expressing compassion or sympathy? Be your own sound engineer by paying attention to your vocal variations and adjusting them to match your content.

Before You Respond, Breathe and Think

I saved this for last because it can be the hardest behavior to practice. It's easy to take a deep breath and let a lovely compliment sink in, right? But when someone criticizes us or expresses disapproval, being "Zen" usually isn't our first response. Most people become reactive. The instant you get triggered, you start to feel physically uncomfortable. Your breathing and heart rate might increase, and your thinking can get a little foggy. These are signs that the reactive emotional part of your brain has hijacked your rational thinking. When that happens, your ability to solve problems and generate innovative possibilities is compromised dramatically.

As soon as you notice that your emotional brain has grabbed the wheel, you need to pull over. That means stop speaking, regulate your breathing and don't take action until your rational mind is back in the driver's seat. The actions and decisions the emotional brain makes tend to be the ones we regret the most because they're not rationally considered responses.

When you feel the emotional fire raging, stop and regroup. You can use techniques like slow, deep breathing to calm yourself so your rational brain can regain control. When you're calm, you can regulate your emotions, identify your triggers, evaluate the situation and reframe people's actions. That allows you to choose a response that makes the best you proud. It also helps you remember that sometimes the best response is no response at all. This can be hard when someone says or does something that's extremely triggering, but with practice, it's possible. You can always respond at a later time, after you've had a chance to rationally think about what happened, consider what might have motivated the person's actions or words and think of something that's actually worth saying.

Guidelines for Difficult Conversations

Prepare

In some situations, winging it's the way to go, but navigating a tough conversation isn't one of them. If you're talking with a friend and the conversation veers into turbulent water, preparing means pausing for thirty seconds before you share your opinion or answer a question.

However, if there's something you need to talk to someone about that you know may be particularly difficult, start your preparation by giving thought to the differences of opinion that might come up and trying to see the situation or circumstances through the other person's eyes. If you can walk a mile in their shoes, even better. Consider how to make your points in ways that invite discussion instead of shutting it down. You may even want to rehearse what you're going to say to make sure you clearly state what you want, why you want it and what the results might be.

Let's say you're working on a project with a co-worker who isn't pulling their weight. If you say, "I've had it with you not doing your fair share of the work," that will probably be the end of the conversation. But if you say, "I'd like you to provide more of your insight. You have so much experience with the problems we're trying to solve that I'm sure we'll have a better outcome with more of your input," they won't feel like you're attacking them. You're giving them the benefit of the doubt, authentically acknowledging their expertise and inviting them to contribute more. With this approach, you'll have a much better chance of a positive outcome.

It's also helpful to make a list of the things the other person might do or say to trigger your emotional brain. And while you're at it, practice staying calm so you can keep your rational mind in the driver's seat.

Be Brief and Specific

We can spend hours talking with a friend or a partner about the mysteries of life, places we want to travel and other pleasurable topics. As the saying goes, time flies when we're having fun. But when we need to have a conversation that won't be enjoyable, it's best to keep it short.

If you're talking to your co-parent about what school your child should attend, asking for a raise, clearing up a misunderstanding or declining someone's request, use strategies that ensure that you get your point across and keep the relationship intact. One of those strategies is being brief. You need to provide context, but don't overexplain or repeat yourself. Below is the formula to follow.

State your purpose:
I want . . .
Offer your rationale:
I want it because . . .
Provide possible outcomes:
I want us to stop fighting so much.
If we find a better way to resolve our differences, we'll all be happier.

As helpful as this formula can be, what's even more important is to remember that you're in the same village. It's hard to make a positive difference when you can't get along with your people.

Acknowledge and Understand
When Bella took Mario to Rome to visit Nonni and decided not to return to New York, Trevor was devastated. His emotional brain was triggered, and instead of trying to figure out how he could still be an active part of his son's life, he was obsessed with how unreasonable and evil Bella was. "We agreed that raising a family together would be part of our legacy, a way to bring more good into the world," Trevor said. "Now what?"

I asked Trevor if he thought it was possible to raise Mario to bring more good into the world even though he and Bella were splitting up. "Theoretically," he said. "But not if I can't stop hating his mother." He shook his head, "She's self-centered, self-absorbed, deceitful, manipulative, but Mario loves her."

Eventually, Trevor accepted that the only way to have a strong relationship with Mario was to stop seeing Bella as a villain. "It was like I had this mental tattoo of her that I couldn't get past, and it stopped me from reaching out to her and from seeing Mario."

Trevor's "mental tattoo" is the perfect metaphor for our judgments about other people—judgments that limit us and limit the impact we're capable of having. We make a judgment and tattoo it in our mind, and it becomes permanent and unchangeable unless we actively work to remove it or change it. That isn't easy to do, but when you acknowledge and understand what the other person is saying or doing, you can change your perspective. When Trevor realized his mental tattoo of Bella's negative qualities was preventing him from seeing anything positive about her, he decided to find a way to remove it. He started by coming up with ten things about her that he honestly thought were positive, including her creativity, independence, intelligence, and physical fitness. This helped him to stop focusing so much on the traits he considered negative, and he committed to adding another word to his positive list every week. Next, he leaned into the exercise by acknowledging the things he was grateful to Bella for, including being a responsible and loving mom and coordinating his video calls with Mario.

When he shared his lists, I told him it was impressive that he pushed himself to come up with ten positive traits *and* ten things he was grateful for. He laughed. "Yeah, and I didn't even include how lucky I am she's making me more patient."

Sure enough, his efforts were making the tattoo fade, but it wasn't until he saw Bella stand up for their son that a more positive tattoo began to take shape. Now in first grade, Mario was participating in his school's recreational basketball team and Trevor had flown in to visit him and see one of his games, but by the end of the first half Mario hadn't been put in the game. While Trevor didn't think it was his place to question the coach, Bella had no problem questioning him. "As the kids were heading for the locker room, Bella reamed out the coach for not putting Mario in," Trevor said. "She was talking so fast in Italian that I couldn't tell what she was saying, but it was embarrassing." He broke into a grin. "Who *does* that?"

During halftime, Trevor said, he couldn't stop thinking about how differently he would have handled the whole thing. "I'd have kept my mouth shut and worked with Mario to help him get better so he'd get into the game without making a scene."

He was also worried that Bella's confrontation with the coach could work against Mario. But when the third quarter started, Mario was in the game.

"What did you *say* to him?" Trevor asked Bella.

She shrugged. "I said, 'What is this, the NBA? Every kid should get a chance to play. Mario's dad came all the way from New York to see him play and you're going to disappoint *both* of them?'"

After the game, the scene kept replaying in Trevor's mind— Bella pointing at the coach and shouting at him in Italian, everyone in the stands watching, feeling like time had stopped. But he was seeing the things he didn't like about Bella in a new light. "The devil tattoo turned into a fearless advocate," he said. "Her fiery temper was part of being a passionate caregiver." When you change the mental tattoo or label that you have for someone, you give yourself a chance to see more of who they are. For Trevor, it also created an opening to leave the legacy he wanted to leave, but in a different way from what he'd planned.

You can't change someone, and you can't always change a situation, but you *can* change the way you see them and communicate with them. Being intellectually curious, humble, and flexible will help you to appreciate other perspectives. Listening closely and expressing yourself clearly will ensure that the people in your village know you respect them and value your relationship. Making the changes to become a better listener and a better communicator will benefit you and help you to strengthen all of your relationships. Like my colleague Derrick Shirley says, "Nothing changes if nothing changes."

IN BRIEF

- Identifying something you want to change is just one part of the process. Next you need to take the steps to make it happen. When you realize you're not fated to act the same way forever, the options to change and improve become available to you.
- To be worthy of a strong village, capitalize on the knowledge that freedom and responsibility are joined at the hip. If you know you're free to change and you don't make improvements, you're essentially choosing not to bring the best version of yourself to your community and running the risk of losing all the benefits those strong relationships provide.
- Hallmarks of healthy relationships include cooperating, negotiating conflict, and offering and asking for help. Whether you're good at these skills often comes down to how well you can actively listen and clearly communicate, because communication

skills are prerequisites for many other relationship skills.

- Reasonable people disagree on a reasonable number of things a reasonable amount of time. And the way people disagree and express themselves can either create credits or debits in the relationship "bank account."
- You can't have strong relationships without good communication.
- If someone is talking and you're thinking about why they're wrong, it takes a tremendous amount of effort to remain silent. But if you open your mind to understand their point of view, staying silent is easy, and chances are you'll learn something. With this approach, far from being a chore, silence is intellectually stimulating.
- The Active Listener's Mantra: mind open, mouth closed.
- Listen to Learn. Curiosity opens your mind and makes you receptive to new ways of thinking. It makes it possible to have strong connections with people you disagree with.
- Since your opinion or way of doing something is just one of many ways, there's no downside to understanding other opinions and approaches. You can only gain by being curious.
- Understanding doesn't mean agreeing. It just means you can see things from someone else's point of view.
- The consensus among researchers is that over 70 percent of all communication is nonverbal.
- The actions and decisions the emotional brain makes tend to be the ones you regret the most.

- Being intellectually curious, humble, and flexible will help you to see and appreciate other perspectives instead of creating mental tattoos and labels that limit your understanding.
- Listening closely and expressing yourself clearly will ensure that the people in your village know that you respect them and value your relationship.

In Chapter Six, we'll cover relationship best practices, including forming flexible expectations, exchanging certainty for curiosity and expanding the space between stimulus and response.

CHAPTER 6

ADOPT RELATIONSHIP
BEST PRACTICES

When Lucas and Maria learned that the vineyard their families had picked grapes in was for sale, they decided to buy it and turn it into a fair-trade business. Friends since they were kids, they were both general managers of successful companies and felt inspired to increase the number of Hispanic-owned wineries. They both wanted to make a positive impact on the industry and were excited that their visions were so aligned.

Once they hired employees, though, things changed. Lucas wanted an equitable environment with less hierarchy, but Maria was convinced that wouldn't work. It didn't take long for them to find out that their leadership and management styles were very different, and the more they each pushed for the "right way," the more tension they created. When Lucas realized that he wasn't going to change Maria's mind and that the strain on their relationship was only getting worse, he scheduled a session with me to try to figure out how things had gone so wrong.

Since miscommunication is often part of disagreements, we began by exploring how he and Maria expressed themselves and how well they listened to each other. "She has no problem telling me exactly what she's thinking, that's for sure," Lucas said. "And listening . . ." He shrugged. "We're not so good at that."

We spent the first sessions working on listening to learn rather than listening to refute or disprove what the other had said, and once Maria felt "heard," the tension eased a little. As Lucas and I worked together to find the root of the problems, it became clear that he and Maria needed to get better at communicating respectfully. But the biggest hurdle they had to jump was learning and using relationship best practices. If they did that, they could reach their business goals and preserve their friendship.

FORM REALISTIC, FLEXIBLE EXPECTATIONS

As Lucas and I focused on best practices, he realized the partnership was strained because he and Maria had different expectations about leadership and employee relations. They'd both been so excited about the new venture that they assumed they were in sync about how to lead their staff. They also assumed that their visions for long-term growth were aligned. Both assumptions were wrong.

Whether you're developing a business relationship, a friendship, or an intimate partnership, you need to share your expectations, learn about the other person's expectations and be willing to compromise and adjust to preserve the relationship. In hindsight, Lucas said he felt foolish for assuming Maria would want to handle human relations the same way he did, but he still thought things should be done his way. So they were locked in a stalemate, and that's where they'd stay unless one of them made a sincere effort to understand the other's point of view. I explained to Lucas that without that understanding, the chances of reaching an agreement with Maria were minuscule.

Relationship best practice number one is behaving with the awareness that your way is one of *many* ways. Many of your expectations were formed by family values, social norms, and societal narratives, so it's important to reexamine them from time to time to see if they still hold true for you. If you think your business partner should behave a certain way or embrace a particular belief, begin by getting clear about why you believe it's so important. If the expectation were fulfilled, what would the outcome be? Once you know what you want to achieve, you can expand your view to include alternative approaches that can accomplish the same objective. Knowing which expectations are most important to you will help you to pick your battles and make creative compromises.

There's a lot of truth to the formula:

Reality – Expectations = Happiness.

While having expectations is normal, the fewer we have, the more open we are to variety, novelty and surprise. So your goal isn't to eliminate expectations. Your goal is to closely look at your expectations and see if they're aligned with who you want to become. Ideally, you'll end up with a relatively short list of healthy, realistic expectations that others can typically meet.

Once you have your list, the onus is on you to share these important expectations instead of hoping others will some- how magically know what you want. If you're approaching an important milestone and you want your friends and family to celebrate with you, tell them what you want the celebration to look like. The idea that others should know what you ex- pect isn't realistic, even if you think it's obvious. There *is* no obvious. You can't expect other people to know what's a big deal for you. It's a nice surprise when they do, but isn't sharing your expectation more effective than wishing and waiting?

How often have you gotten what you wanted without asking for it or telling someone you wanted it? What's clear as glass in *your* mind can be clear as marble to somebody else. If you expect something, communicate your expectation ahead of time. Saying, "You should have known I wanted to work on that project," or, "It should have been obvious I wanted jewelry for our anniversary," after you don't get those things isn't helpful, and it's not good for the relationship. The statement "If I tell someone what I want, it won't mean as much if they give it to me" is absurd. If you're setting yourself up for disappointment like that, please stop. If you have an expectation, say so. Not with a hint but with a straightforward announcement or request. If you expect your employees or co-workers to be on time for meetings, make that clear. If you expect to be considered for an opening at work, express your interest.

Sharing expectations is a powerful way to keep your relationships healthy. Just keep in mind that it's a two-way street. You share your expectations, the other person shares theirs, and with the willingness to adjust what you each expect, you meet somewhere in between. To do this, determine what you want or need, clearly communicate your expectation and be ready to adjust, like in the following examples:

Example 1

1. You expect your employees to be inspired by your vision to become a carbon-neutral company.
2. You share your vision with your employees, but it doesn't motivate them as much as you'd expected.

3. You learn that your employees are more motivated by money, titles, and praise, so to reach your goal to become a carbon-neutral company, you adjust your expectations and provide motivation in the form that works for them.

Example 2

1. You expect to hike up Machu Picchu on your vacation.
2. You tell your travel companions about this desire as you start planning for the trip, but a few of your friends don't have the physical endurance to do the hike.
3. You adjust your expectations and opt for taking the train up to the ruins and walk only the last part of the trail instead.

Example 3

1. You expect your business partner to reinvest all dividends in the company for the first five years because it's "obvious" that that's what's needed for the company to grow.
2. You share this expectation with your partner and she agrees.
3. Your partner finds out she's carrying twins and will need more income than expected, so you change the original formula so that only half of the dividends will be reinvested for the first five years.

Example 4

1. You expect to continue living in your hometown, where your family and friends live.

2. Before you get married, you share this expectation with your partner.
3. Your partner's company offers him a big promotion that involves moving, so you shift your original expectation for the good of the relationship.

The ability to adjust expectations is essential in relationships because there are bound to be surprises, both good and bad, along the way.

YOUR TRUTH IS MOSTLY SUBJECTIVE

Once Maria understood that Lucas wanted to manage the company from a "people first" perspective in order to right the wrongs their parents had endured and pioneer a new business model for successful vineyards, she stopped thinking her way was the only way and worked with him to find solutions they could both embrace. But he still had a hard time with her tendency to think the worst when somebody made a mistake. "She says she understands that everyone makes mistakes, but when someone makes one, she assumes they were being careless or not paying attention," Lucas said. "She never cuts anyone slack."

As Lucas dug deeper to learn why Maria was so critical, he found out that getting employees to follow the procedures at her other company was a constant battle. "The crap people pull is crazy," he said, shaking his head. "Now I get why she thinks my approach is too soft. I still think it's right, but I'm willing to meet her halfway."

Sometimes, choosing not to do what you think is "right" is the better way to go. Norms, rules, beliefs, morals, and standards all change over time, and they differ around the world.

So "right" is relative and reality isn't concrete, because we perceive everything from our unique point of view. A point of view is literally a view from a specific point, and everything can be seen from a full circle of specific points. If two people standing on opposite sides of a street see a car crash, they'll have different perspectives on what happened. If a third person sees the crash from a second-story window, *their* perspective will be different from the other two. We could chalk this up to the fact that some people are better at remembering details than others, but the same thing happens with cameras. When referees review the recording of a play that's in question, they look at it from multiple camera angles. What seems obvious from one angle isn't clear from another.

This same analogy holds true when people have different intellectual, philosophical, religious or political points of view. Our beliefs, which are essentially points of view, are affected by our identities, including how we identify socially, culturally, emotionally, sexually, spiritually, religiously, financially, and intellectually. The factors and beliefs that contribute to our individuality also mold our truth. Dan Thurmon, author of *Off Balance on Purpose,* says reality itself is subjective: ". . . We don't live a fact-based existence. We process the world through our emotions."[1] When we look through that lens, we can make peace with uncertainty and use our curiosity and empathy to understand people who have different points of view. With this approach, we can embrace our truth without feeling the need to make other people wrong or wasting time trying to refute their reality. We all have unique versions of reality and Thurman says that's okay: "Extend empathy as you actively shape an inspiring reality that is all your own."

Because individual beliefs and experiences inform your truth and color your reality, it just follows that most "truth" is subjective. In other words, what's good or right for you may be bad or wrong for someone else and vice versa. Consider these examples of subjective truth:

- Music, painting, and literature. Does commercial success equal good art? If you love a song or a book or a painting and someone else can't stand it, is it good or bad?
- The definition of success. Is it a high salary? Being free to do what you love? Living authentically?
- What happens after we die? Nothing, game over? Resurrection? Reincarnation? Something else?

No matter what your truth is, instead of defending it, try to increase your understanding of what others think is true. Being argumentative builds walls. Being curious and interested builds bridges.

EXCHANGE CERTAINTY FOR CURIOSITY

The Greek philosopher Protagoras said the way we interpret every experience, or anything at all, is relative to each one of us.[2] More than twenty-five hundred years ago in ancient Greece, that idea was revolutionary and widely debated. His theory was often translated as "Man is the measure of all things." For example, if a room were sixty-five degrees Fahrenheit, it would feel cold to someone who'd just stepped out of a hot shower and hot to someone who'd just come in from a snowstorm. Protagoras's perspective was that both people were correct based on their own experience and interpretation. So when we think something is right or wrong, or in this case hot or cold, it's helpful to understand that it may be both. But a few decades after Protagoras put forth his theory, the Greek philosopher Plato argued that there had to be an ultimate truth—otherwise, every dispute over right and wrong would simply be opinion. He also said laws and social customs would be meaningless if we didn't have ultimate truths. Plato was so passionate about his position that he wrote a fictional philosophical dialogue with Protagoras that contradicted the philosopher's relativist view.

No matter what philosophy you subscribe to, there *are* truths that aren't subjective. If, for example, you don't believe in gravity, you'll still fall to the ground if you step off a roof. But in most situations, acknowledging possibilities other than your own point of view is the most harmonious way to move forward. It doesn't mean you believe a different truth—it means you're open-minded enough to recognize that subjective truths are interesting to learn and usually not worth arguing about. As Steven Levitt and Stephen Dubner say in *Think Like a Freak*, "Being confident you are right is not the same as being right." Even if a particular perspective could be right, attempting to prove it comes at the cost of making other people wrong. Nobody likes that, and it won't change their minds. When we press a point, we make the divide bigger. When we're curious about someone else's perspective, we can narrow the divide.

Curiosity—the strong desire to learn something—can lead us to increase our understanding of any topic and even motivate us to learn just for the sake of knowledge itself. You may be thinking, *But didn't curiosity kill the cat?* Probably not. Or at least not as often as the expression might suggest. The original version of the saying appeared in 1598 in English playwright Ben Jonson's *Every Man in His Humour*: "Helter skelter, hang sorrow, care'll kill a cat . . ." At the time "care" was a synonym for "worry" or "sorrow for others." A year later, in *Much Ado About Nothing*, Shakespeare wrote, "What though care killed a cat, thou hast mettle enough in thee to kill care." How and where the expression morphed into "Curiosity killed the cat" isn't known, but the modern version is meant to warn us against the dangers of being too inquisitive and snooping around.

My take is that curiosity didn't kill the cat, it made the cat smarter and better because being curious motivates us to explore our environment so we can learn and develop. All animals are curious. It's an innate behavior. The human desire for knowledge itself is called epistemic curiosity, and a study conducted in Germany showed that this type of curiosity "facilitates the acquisition of knowledge by promoting reasoning."

The study, "Being snoopy and smart: The relationship between curiosity, fluid intelligence, and knowledge," concluded: "One might speculate that epistemically curious individuals enrich their environment, which in turn enhances their cognitive ability."[3] Because curiosity leads to understanding and empathy, it can improve relationships and fuel success. It's proven to be a positive motivational system that's more important than certainty, and some companies are including curiosity in their employee selection process. The design and consulting company IDEO, for example, looks for people with skills that qualify them to actively engage in the creative process and collaborate well across disciplines. This requires curiosity and empathy, which are related.

In the article "The Business Case for Curiosity" in the *Harvard Business Review*, behavioral scientist and Harvard Business School professor Francesca Gino says IDEO understands that "empathy allows employees to listen thoughtfully and see problems or decisions from another person's perspective, while curiosity extends to interest in other people's disciplines, so much so that one may start to practice them."[4] She says IDEO also believes that being a specialist isn't what makes most people perform well—it's the fact that their curiosity prompts them to explore, ask questions, and collaborate with others.

In 2004 Google leased a billboard in Silicon Valley and anonymously posted: "{first 10-digit prime found in consecutive digits of e}.com." The curious people who figured out the answer—7427466391.com—and visited the website were presented with another equation. Then Google invited the handful of people who solved that one to submit their résumés. Gino says Google used this approach because it "places a high premium on curiosity." The company also asks interview questions that help to identify people who are naturally curious, such as "Have you ever found yourself unable to stop learning something you've never encountered before, and if so, why?" Some said they were required to keep learning because it was their job to find an answer, but others said they kept going simply because they were curious.

In a study that Gino conducted with 120 employees, she found that when people are curious, they look at difficult situations more creatively than when they're not. "I found that natural curiosity was associated with better job performance, as evaluated by their direct bosses," she says. Scientists have also learned that when curious people are under stress or provoked, they tend to be less defensive than others.

With a curiosity mindset, you can formulate a variety of explanations for why people behave in ways you find annoying or upsetting. That can help you understand and navigate other people's behaviors instead of reacting emotionally and potentially damaging relationships. Gino's research results also show that curiosity helps people work well with others. "My research found that curiosity encourages members of a group to put themselves in one another's shoes and take an interest in one another's ideas rather than focus only on their own perspective," she says. "That causes them to work together more effectively and smoothly: Conflicts are less heated, and groups achieve better results."

If you're not naturally curious, one of the best ways to develop this trait is to be humble about what you think you know. People who think they have all the answers don't question much, so they may not learn much. On the other hand, when you acknowledge that you only possess a tiny fraction of the knowledge that exists, it's intellectually humbling, and not only is that humility key to curiosity but it also makes it easier to start new relationships and maintain the ones you have.

Tenelle Porter, assistant professor of educational psychology at Ball State University, says intellectual humility is acknowledging that our knowledge is incredibly limited. The research she conducted as a postdoctoral scholar showed that people with higher levels of intellectual humility tend to be more willing to consider opinions and points of view that differ from their own. The study also indicated that people with more intellectual humility perform better at work and in school. Porter says that when we understand there's so much we don't know, we're more likely to see the world as ever-changing and function with the awareness that the future will be different from the present. "By embracing this insight, leaders and employees can begin to recognize the power of exploration."[5]

While researchers have only been scientifically studying intellectual humility for about a decade, the results are already encouraging. "It has been variously described as a remedy for political polarization, a tool for advancing scientific credibility, and a disposition that promotes learning," Porter says. In her studies, she found that people who were aware of the limits of their own knowledge disagreed more constructively, appreciated the intellectual strengths of others and were more receptive to learning about opposing views. In a divided and polarized world, intellectual humility and curiosity are some of the most valuable traits we can develop. They can help us to engage instead of defend, and this has the potential to lead to a more harmonious and peaceful world.

Cultivate Curiosity

We can all cultivate curiosity. Here are a few ways to begin:

- Ask why. Question everything. A fool isn't the person who asks a question but the one who doesn't. Challenge yourself to be the person who asks questions more than you share answers. You already know what you know—how about finding out what other people know?
- Widen your horizons. Talk to people who have different views, values and perspectives from your own. See if you can understand why they have the view and positions they have. Challenge yourself to "get" their point of view.
- Observe and explore. Engage with the world, the people around you and nature. Allow yourself to wander through a bookstore, stop in a different coffee shop, people-watch and eavesdrop. Curiosity requires time. It's an unfolding process. Wonder how things came to be.

- Try new things, including foods, sports, hobbies, music and literature. There are so many things to experience in the world, and a wider range of experiences in a variety of realms will feed your curiosity and spark more questions.
- Focus on the future. "I've always done things this way" doesn't mean there isn't a different and maybe more enjoyable way to do it. How will you know if you don't try?
- Take a childlike approach to life. As adults we tend to think we know a lot, and even when we know that we don't know, ego can stop us from asking questions and exploring.

Increase Your Intellectual Humility

Intellectual humility stems from a desire to learn more and figure out what's true, even if it means changing your opinion or shifting your stance—or, to put it less politely, admitting you're wrong. Here are a few ways to begin:

- Cultivate a growth mindset. To learn more, you have to be willing to admit you don't know everything. A growth mindset is about recognizing that you have room to grow intellectually.
- Reframe difficulties as opportunities to learn and grow. This will create great opportunities to learn something new.
- Say, "I don't know." Getting comfortable with that means you're secure enough to acknowledge that you don't know everything and that not knowing some things doesn't diminish the things you do know.

EXPAND THE SPACE BETWEEN
STIMULUS AND RESPONSE

After several months of practicing new relationship skills, Lucas's relationship with Maria was steadily improving, but there were still some things that were emotionally triggering. "When I'm talking and she rolls her eyes, I want to break something," he told me.

"So what do you do when you have that knee-jerk reaction?" I said.

"I do what my grandma taught me when I was a kid: count to ten and don't do or say anything. But with Maria, my head feels like it's about to explode."

I assured Lucas that he could learn to feel a little less triggered each time she rolled her eyes but that it would take practice. Learning to stretch out the space between what happens and your response is a practice that some people never learn. If you know someone like this, you've seen the negative effects their knee-jerk reactions have on their relationships and their success, and you can use that as motivation to avoid those mistakes yourself.

I encouraged Lucas to start noticing how he felt when he was triggered and to replay and explore these events afterward. "Notice where you feel the anger starting," I said. "Does your heart start to race? Do your palms get sweaty? Do you feel mentally foggy or flustered? Try to identify the physical 'tells' that let you know your emotions are ramping up."

Once you can identify these initial feelings, you can predict and change your reaction. If you're thinking that's easier said than done, you're right. It won't happen overnight. It will take vigilance and practice and at first you'll probably fail. And then you'll probably fail again. But just becoming aware of the opening between action and reaction is a win. The more conscious you become of this space, the easier it will be for you to recognize that you can choose your reaction.

When a client tells me about something they did or said that they regret, I ask them when they felt like they were losing control. If they mentally replay the scene, they can usually identify this point. And with increased awareness, they learn to identify the moment they're about to lose control *as* it's happening. As soon as they recognize they're triggered, they can take a breath and stop themselves from saying or doing something they may regret. Sometimes. The knee-jerk reaction can be stubborn and take a while to retrain, so failing is part of the learning process. But with practice you can learn to use the space between stimulus and response as an opportunity to avoid regret and influence the outcome of the interaction.

Your power lies in identifying whatever precedes your knee-jerk and heading it off at the pass. Identifying this moment is key because if you know when you're about to react emotionally, you can hit pause, take a breath and center yourself. That allows you to de-escalate, think rationally, decide how you want to interpret what happened, and respond in a way that reflects the best you.

If someone says something you find insulting try this three-step approach:

1. Notice your initial impulse
2. Expand the space
3. Choose how to act

Below are a few examples.

1. Notice your initial impulse:
   - Physical: Feel your heart thumping in your chest.
   - Emotional: *I want to return the insult and throw this plate at you.*

2. Expand the space:
   - Physical: Take long, slow breaths.
   - Mental (thought process, analysis): Remind yourself of the person you want to be. *The person I want to be doesn't insult people or throw plates.*

3. Choose how to act:
   - Physical: Disengage. Put the plate down and walk away without saying anything. Return to the conversation after rationally (not reactively) thinking about the best way to proceed.

If you're having a hard time calming down, maybe go for a run or a long walk, meditate or do something else that's healthy and will make you feel better. Everyone's strategy for moving from negative emotions back to balance and positive emotions is unique. Take the time to formulate an effective strategy that includes a variety of options that you know will work for you. If you're not sure, experiment until you do know.

When you're practicing stretching the space between stimulus and response, it helps to think about actions as proactive and responses as reactive. If someone is being rude or unfair or generally pushing your buttons, feeling an emotional knee-jerk reaction is as normal as your leg jerking up when a doctor gives that spot below your knee a sharp tap. But unlike a physical knee jerk, you can control what you say and do, even when you're emotionally triggered. When you stretch the space between what happens and your response, you can wisely choose your next step. In time, you'll realize you're not a prisoner of your emotions. You always have the freedom and space to choose a response that's characteristic of who you aspire to be.

In the 1963 article "Freedom and Responsibility Re-Examined," American existential psychologist Rollo May said, "Indeed I would define mental health as the capacity to be aware of the gap between stimulus and response, together with the capacity to use this gap constructively." And twelve years later in *The Courage to Create*, May said, "Human freedom involves our capacity to pause between stimulus and response and, in that pause, to choose the one response toward which we wish to throw our weight. The capacity to create ourselves, based on this freedom, is inseparable from consciousness or self-awareness."

The space between stimulus and response is one of the most valuable pieces of real estate we have. People who don't make good use of this space are making their lives more difficult than they need to be. How many times have you blurted out something that you immediately regretted or lost your temper and made someone feel bad when it could have been avoided? Most people squander the freedom the space provides, but wouldn't life be more interesting and joyful if you carefully considered how to respond instead of reacting impulsively? Knee-jerk reactions were designed for life-and-death situations, like ducking when you hear a loud noise. They're great for survival, but if you let your triggered emotions determine your reactions, you're forfeiting your freedom to choose.

Without this understanding, people are easily held hostage

by their own emotions. "I can't help how I feel" is a widely accepted myth. In truth, our feelings are based on our beliefs, perceptions, and experiences, and we can change them just like we can change behaviors that aren't serving our purpose or helping us to be our best selves. If you master the art of expanding the space between stimulus and response and carefully choose your actions and words, all of your relationships will improve.

IN BRIEF

- Whether you're developing a business relationship, a friendship or an intimate partnership, you need to share your expectations, learn about the other person's expectations, and be willing to compromise and adjust to preserve the relationship.
- Relationship best practice number one is behaving with the awareness that your way is one of *many* ways.
- Sharing expectations is a powerful way to keep your relationships healthy.
- "Right" is relative and reality isn't concrete, because you perceive everything from your unique point of view.
- No matter what your truth is, instead of defending it, try to increase your understanding of what others think is true. Being argumentative builds walls. Being interested in what others believe builds bridges.

- When you press a point, you make the divide bigger. When you're curious about someone else's perspective, you can narrow the divide.
- Because curiosity leads to understanding and empathy, it can improve relationships and fuel success.
- When you acknowledge that you only possess a tiny fraction of the knowledge that exists, it's intellectually humbling, and not only is that humility key to curiosity but it also makes it easier to start new relationships and maintain the ones you have.
- When you're trying to stretch the space between stimulus and response, it helps to think about actions as proactive and responses as reactive.
- The space between stimulus and response is one of the most valuable assets you have.

In Chapter Seven, you'll learn how to build a strong village that can help you make a lasting impact.

CHAPTER 7

BUILD YOUR VILLAGE

When Work Coherence's chief purpose officer was a teenager, she became curious about why some people were almost always happy and others weren't. Lara Bezerra knew she wanted to be one of the happy ones but didn't know how to achieve that goal, so she asked her mother, who was both a physicist and an MD. Surely she'd have an answer.

And she did, but it wasn't the one Lara was looking for. "Stop looking for ways to be happy," her mother said. "If you want to be happy, just be happy. It's a choice."

"At the time, that didn't sound possible," Lara says, so she asked her grandfather why *he* was happy most of the time. "Happiness comes from wisdom," he said. "Normally, people get wiser when they're older, so they have a short time to be happy. The younger you get wiser, the more time you'll have to be happy."

That didn't really make sense to Lara, but it sounded like something she could do, so she became more diligent about her studies. Throughout high school and college, she set high standards for herself, and before she'd even completed her bachelor's degree in business administration, she landed her first job as a sales trainee at Janssen Inc. And five years later, at age twenty-seven, she was promoted to sales administration manager.

"My mother and grandfather gave me advice that helped me to make good choices," Lara says, "and because they believed in me, I believed in myself. They were the first members of my personal board of directors."

Whether we call it a board of directors, a dream team or a village, research studies and empirical evidence make a powerful case for actively developing relationships with people who want to help us succeed. Not everyone is fortunate enough to grow up with a supportive village, but those who do often have a considerable advantage. As Lara was finding her footing as a leader, her personal board of directors was right there to support her, especially her mom, who began reading books about business and leadership so she could gain a better understanding of what her daughter was experiencing. They had long talks about what it meant to be a good leader, and for Lara it meant being authentic, but that wasn't lining up with what her supervisors were recommending. "My bosses were telling me not to get close to employees or bring too much personal life to my professional life," she says.

That didn't work for Lara. She didn't believe in separating her business life from her personal life. She was the same person no matter what environment she was in or who she was interacting with. So instead of keeping a distance from employees, she learned about their lives outside work and supported their goals and well-being. She didn't want to enforce her power—she wanted to be a positive influence they respected. And because she was, they all worked together to integrate market intelligence and sales force efficiency and implement career planning and incentive systems, which were new processes and practices in the 1990s. And since she was so successful in Brazil she was asked to implement the same systems in Portugal.

She didn't want to accept the transfer, though. Her mother, Masa, had a cardiac problem and her doctor said she didn't have long to live. But Masa put her foot down. "You have to go and take the job," she told Lara. "If you stay here, I'll feel like I have to die sooner. Go to Portugal and I'll visit you there."

So Lara accepted the position and her mother kept her promise.

BE WHO YOU ARE

In Portugal, Lara's role as sales administration manager was to finalize the implementation of sales automatization. To make the process work, the logistics department had to restructure its process because it was the bottleneck for the final implementation. "I had ideas for how to restructure the logistics department," Lara says, "but instead of making that decision, I helped the department review the process, and they came up with great suggestions that I took to the head of the company." He was so pleased with the collaborative effort and creative solutions that he asked Lara to stay another year to help the controlling department. "This is when I learned how effective it was to empower people to be themselves and be willing to express their thoughts and ideas," Lara says.

Many studies have shown a link between authenticity and well-being, but a study conducted by researchers from the University of Nebraska showed that authenticity also improves the workplace.[1] The participants said it saves time and energy and improves productivity and performance because they don't have to "hide themselves."

Lara's approach was so successful that after she worked in the controlling department for a year, she was asked to go to the global headquarters in Germany to prepare employees to step into higher positions within the company. "In Germany, just like in Portugal and Brazil, I stressed the importance of authenticity, wellness and trust," she says. "We worked well together and helped each other achieve the goals we'd set."

The goals Lara was achieving as one of the European Union business managers didn't go unnoticed. Because of her dedication and track record, less than two years later she was offered the position of general manager of pharmaceuticals at Bayer Hungary. While she was GM, she also reopened Bayer's Slovakian affiliate and became the general manager there, too. So by her mid-thirties, Lara was managing companies in two countries.

In Hungary, Lara was eager to learn how to be a better leader from her team members, who were older and more experienced than she was. "It was here that I learned the importance of authenticity, asking for help in leading, and learning from the team," she says. "And at the same time, I was bringing meditation and other exercises for us to learn together. Not as their leader but as a member of the team." She built strong connections by promoting trust, life balance, and well-being. "In Hungarian, the word *bizalom* means 'trust,' and that's what I prioritized from my first day in Hungary."

But it wasn't easy and it wasn't fast. It took two years for Lara to bring the team together, and the path was far from rosy. "That's when I reread the *The Servant: A Simple Story About the True Essence of Leadership*, by James C. Hunter, which my mother gave me when I was promoted to general manager. When she gave it to me, she said, 'This is the kind of leader you should aim to be.'"

Hunter's message is that true leadership isn't about using power. It's about building trust by helping the people we're leading, having authentic relationships with them, loving them and being willing to make sacrifices for them. "That book helped me see that I could lead a profitable company and achieve better results by helping employees to be stronger and working toward a shared purpose."

She says that the book gave her the confidence to continue being a coherent leader and that when the team did finally come together, it was because they'd learned to trust each other. They'd built a village with that trust and a shared purpose to work ethically and be the example in Hungary's pharmaceutical market. So when they faced the challenge of integrating Hungary's market with the Eurozone, they were positioned to succeed.

And succeed they did. Under Lara's leadership, her team standardized ethical, regulatory, and other policies in the Hungarian office without causing the kind of conflict and turmoil that can go hand in hand with major changes.

"The sales results and profitability proved that following a code of ethics could improve results and profits, and our clients appreciated doing business with an ethical company," Lara says. Once again, developing authentic connections had proved to be a win-win. She smiles and her eyes twinkle when she says, "*Bizalom!*"

Watching her team thrive strengthened her belief that being an authentic, coherent leader and making it safe for employees to be themselves is the best way to run a company or organization. It also shed light on the advice her mother gave her back in her teens. "By that time, I understood that we can choose happiness, and being a leader helped me learn how to help other people be happy."

While Lara's style of leadership was uncommon at the time, we now know that fostering trust and authenticity isn't a "soft" skill—it's an essential element of a company's success. In a 2013 study, researchers at Utrecht University in the Netherlands concluded that most employees believe authenticity at work leads to greater productivity as well as better relationships with co-workers, higher trust levels and a more positive working environment all around.[2] And a study conducted by Jensen and Luthans at the University of Nebraska says, "Employees' perception of authentic leadership serves as the strongest predictor of job satisfaction and can have a positive impact on work-related attitudes and happiness."

After five years as a GM, Lara was asked to manage sales and marketing operations for all of Latin America. But again, she had reservations about pulling up stakes. "I had some fear about going to Latin America after eight years in Europe. A lot had changed." Her mother had died two years earlier, and instead of going to Mexico for the new position, Lara wanted to go back to Brazil to be near her family. And if it hadn't been for her village, that's exactly what she would have done.

Her boss, who had never led her wrong, said the position was a great opportunity and urged her to accept it. Two colleagues who were CEOs also encouraged her to take the job because it could open doors to higher positions. And her sister and brother were all for it too even though they missed her as much as she missed them. "You know what Mama would say?" her brother, Marcelo, said. "She'd tell you that if something is appearing in front of you, it's because they need you there. So you have to take this chance. You don't know what good things will happen for you there."

She knew Marcelo was right, but she still had doubts, so she called a mentor who'd encouraged her to accept the GM position in Hungary and had been supportive during her mother's passing. Christa was a long-standing member of Lara's personal board of directors and they'd become friends over the years. Like the others, Christa encouraged her to accept Bayer's offer, making it unanimous. Lara decided to go.

"Because I'd been motivated by fear, I was just looking at a few of my choices," she says. "But my board of directors opened up choices that I would never have seen."

When we're genuine and coherent, we can develop strong authentic connections that make it safe to confide our fears, admit mistakes and share our loftiest aspirations. When we're vulnerable, our village can offer the best guidance and support because they know us well and they know what we hope for and what we fear. That type of insightful input can help us to make better decisions, stretch our comfort zones and reach our goals faster. "Listening to the people I trust instead of my own fears was one of the best things I've ever done," Lara says. Not only was Christa right about the move's being a steppingstone, but while Lara was in Mexico she reconnected with and married a former boyfriend. Five years later, they adopted their three children in Venezuela, finally making Lara's dream to be a mother come true.

"There are moments in your life when you're mostly afraid," Lara says. "Your fear is very big and you have to make a decision. Normally these are the moments that we don't share with anybody because we don't want to show our vulnerability. We want to be strong. And in wanting to be strong, we can make decisions based on our fears. I would have gone home to Brazil if I hadn't shared my fears with my private board. But I did the right thing by having the right people in my life, not only helping me to make a wise decision but opening up an infinite window of opportunity that I was about to close."

Strong connections can enrich your life in every possible way, including helping you to become a better version of yourself. Your village will expand your potential with their knowledge and experience *and* encourage you to take calculated risks for the sake of following your dreams and making the impact you want to make.

CHOOSE YOUR VILLAGERS WISELY

When you build a village, you create a place where you belong. In addition to filling a basic human need, having these close connections can help you to achieve the goals that you've set. So for your adult village, assemble a group of people who are as wise and supportive as Lara's personal board. Actively develop relationships with emotionally mature people who appreciate who you are, cheer you on and believe in your ability to make a lasting impact.

As you think about who you want to have in your village, consider people who can help you through major transitions and people who understand you well enough to anticipate potential hurdles and be ready to help you over them. When my client Lee got out of rehab, he was looking forward to playing golf again but worried about the tradition of being offered a shot of bourbon after scoring a birdie. Lee had one of the lowest handicaps in his league, so it was only a matter of time before he'd face this moment, and sure enough, the first time back on the course he birdied the third hole. "The birdie gets the worm," his friend said without missing a beat and handed him a purple gummy worm. For Lee, that six-inch piece of candy was worth more than gold. If you have people like this in your village, consider yourself blessed.

Ideally, you'll build a village with about fifteen people, and a handful of them will be like a village council. Not everyone in your village needs to excel in all areas of friendship. If your village is built with diversity, everyone can express his or her unique brilliance.

Your Villagers Can Be:

1. Friends who are part of your inner circle. You can always count on them. They're reliable, loyal, and supportive. They're happy when things are going your way and quick to lend a hand when they're not. They know you well, and when you share a problem or something you're struggling with, they offer helpful ideas and insights.

2. Friends who are cheerleaders. They support you in everything you decide to do, coming to every play, concert and presentation. They're full of unwavering optimism and believe in you even when you don't believe in yourself.

3. Friends who serve as a moral compass. They may be further along on their spiritual, financial or philosophical journeys than you are and can provide wise counsel or just set an inspiring example. They believe you can achieve and even exceed your goals, and they support your growth and success.

4. People you see often because of proximity or common interests, such as family members, neighbors and co-workers.

5. People in groups you belong to, like golf leagues, book clubs or sports teams.

Some villagers will be in your life for the duration and others for a specific time period, like a mentor, the parents of your kids' best friends or someone who's going through a similar experience.

Your Village Council

These are "your people"—your best friends and those you turn to for guidance about various aspects of life. They're usually people in the top three categories above, but there can be exceptions. Aim to have two or three council members, but having even just one can make a huge difference. So many of my clients who have faced difficult situations managed to pull through and eventually thrive because of that one person who believed in them and was always there for them. If you don't have people in your inner circle who are like Lara's board members, now's the time to start developing those relationships.

Exercise: Identify Your Villagers and Council Members

1. Refer back to the people you listed on your Relationship Roster in Chapter Three.
2. For each person on the list, note the positive influence they have on you, whether it's motivating or inspiring you, encouraging you to pursue your dreams or anything else they do to add something meaningful to your life.
3. Circle the names of one to three people you think of as council members.

If there are people who used to be valued members of your village but you've drifted apart or parted ways, consider whether you want to repair or remodel those relationships. Even the best relationships aren't rustproof, and many things can cause erosion. Maybe you were taking each other for granted or getting on each other's nerves, or maybe there was envy or a lot of backhanded comments and snide remarks. Whatever the situations were, if there are people you want to reconnect with, there are things you can do to potentially reignite the respect and generosity that brought you together once upon a time.

Sometimes it's a matter of understanding that life got in the way. Between work, raising kids and juggling other obligations, we can behave in ways that aren't our best. In a situation like this, maybe all it will take to get the relationship back on track is to agree to reinvent it with the current realities of life. When a relationship falters, many times it's not either person's fault. There's a wrench in the operation that has to be removed.

NOT ALL RELATIONSHIPS CAN BE REPAIRED

Unfortunately, not every relationship can be remodeled or repaired. Sometimes disconnecting is the only healthy choice. Tara Westover, author of *Educated*, didn't begin her own education until she was seventeen. Instead of attending high school, she and her siblings prepared for the "end of days" while isolated from the rest of the world on a mountain in Idaho. They stockpiled emergency supplies, weapons, gold and fuel, they bottled peaches and they made tinctures from plants because their parents forbade the use of medicine. Their father distrusted the government and was convinced that the FBI was out to get them, and Tara had no way of knowing that the world beyond her family's property was anything other than what her father said it was. It wasn't until she learned about bipolar disorder that she started to make some sense of her father's paranoia.

Tara, who found textbooks to help her prepare for college entrance exams and was accepted by Brigham Young University even though she hadn't attended high school, says in *Educated* that she used her childhood journals to write about her journey of reclaiming "custody of my own mind." In addition to "unlearning" the false beliefs her father had instilled, she tried to come to terms with the physical abuse her brother Shawn had inflicted. When she confronted her parents about it, instead of acknowledging that they could have done better or holding Shawn accountable, they demonized Tara. Her family's denial of her reality was so forceful that "I actually believed that I was crazy," she says. "[My parents] succeeded in making me not trust myself in any meaningful way. It's very difficult to continue to believe in yourself and that you're a good person when the people who know you best don't."

Tara, who went on to win a visiting fellowship at Harvard while earning her doctorate in history from Trinity College, Cambridge, says that for a long time she felt like something was wrong with her. She was ashamed that her parents didn't love her, and she thought writing her memoir might remove some shame for other people who'd experienced similar isolation and rejection. While many people would be angry with their family for the rest of their lives, Tara said in an article in *The Irish Times* that she's not angry anymore, because she's no longer under their power and no longer afraid.[3] "You can love someone and still choose to say goodbye to them, and you could miss someone every day and still be glad they're not in your life," she said.

This is one of the saddest truths to accept, so I help my clients explore their options for healing and rebuilding relationships before they arrive at this conclusion. We all say and do things we aren't proud of—that's part of being human—but when someone's dominant personality is negative or they don't have enough self-control to avoid hurting others, they're jeopardizing your village and your chances of leaving a legacy. In these relationships, 1 + 1 = less than 2.

Exercise: How Strong Is Your Connection?

It's not always clear when it's time to end a relationship, but here are some questions you can explore to guide this difficult decision:

1. Does the other person only call when they need something—money, support, a favor, an ear?
2. Does the person usually call to tell you news that will destabilize you or share news or gossip that's negative?
3. Do they belittle your accomplishments or turn them into non-accomplishments? When you share an accomplishment, do they "one-up" you?
4. Do they spread gossip and/or try to involve you in dramas you have no interest in?

5. Do you feel guilty or inadequate when you're around
    them? Do you feel like you always need to explain
    yourself and/or defend yourself?
6. Do you often have unproductive arguments? Feel
    gaslighted?
7. Do you feel like you're dealing with an opponent
    instead of a friend or partner?

If you answered yes to three or more of these questions,
seriously consider whether the relationship is doing more
harm than good—and whether to rescue the relationship or
disconnect. If you love someone or you're attached to them,
you may try to make excuses for their unhealthy behavior because the thought of disconnecting is too painful. But if you sit
quietly and allow yourself to be objective, you may see that the
pain you're trying to avoid is less harmful than the pain you're
enduring.

Your goal in this exercise is to gain clarity about how to
move forward with relationships that aren't working. You may
find it with objective analysis, meditation, prayer, a walk in
the woods or by talking about it with your village council. I
also recommend setting a time limit for making the decision.
If you're having a hard time deciding or you're struggling with
the decision you've made, consider adding a therapist to your
village.

FORTIFY YOUR VILLAGE

You can make your village stronger by including people with a variety of strengths and talents and diverse backgrounds and beliefs. It can also be particularly helpful to include people who disagree with you. People who respectfully disagree can broaden your view and help you reexamine your opinions, just like US Supreme Court Justices Scalia and Ginsburg helped strengthen each other's arguments by explaining why they disagreed. If you surround yourself only with "yes people," you miss the opportunity to enhance your understanding of other valid points of view. Learning about different perspectives gives you the option to shift your point of view or strengthen your convictions with better evidence. Either way it's a win.

Fortifying your village means taking the initiative to strengthen your connections and show people how valuable they are to you. This includes being proactive about maintaining these relationships, often over time and across long distances. If you don't keep your connections strong, you may not feel comfortable asking for guidance or insight when you need it the most, and that can cost you dearly.

If Lara hadn't continued to develop her relationship with Christa, she may have turned down the opportunity that paved the way for starting her own company. Over the years, Christa helped Lara to make big decisions at some of the most challenging crossroads of her life, both personally and professionally. So when Roche offered Lara a CEO position in Venezuela, Christa was the first person she called. "I wanted to do something different, and I thought Roche could allow me to deepen my leadership role the way that I wanted," Lara says. "But Bayer made me who I was, so I had a lot of doubts about leaving. It was Christa who gave me the clarity and peace of mind that I needed to take that big step."

Five years later when Lara was offered the CEO position at Roche in India, once again it was her village that encouraged her to accept the challenge. "It was in India where all of the things I'd been learning and practicing came together," she says. "When I first told one of the directors about the style of leadership I used, he said, 'That will never work in India'. And I said, 'Maybe I believe in your people more than you do.'" As it turned out, it did work. Lara created a strong village by seeing potential in everyone and encouraging them to be their best and help each other to do the same. In just two years the reputation of the company turned around. With national media mentioning the work Roche India was doing, the engagement rate increased from 40 percent to 86 percent, sales increased and negotiations were underway with stakeholders to improve health care in India and bring new medicines to the country.

———————

Exercise: Assess Your Relationships' Potential

Exploring your relationships' potential can open a whole new world. For each person on your Relationship Roster, answer the following questions:

1. How do they support my life purpose and goals, and how do I support theirs?

2. What do I find most valuable about them, and what do they find most valuable about me?
3. How do they motivate me to do better and be better, and how do I motivate them to do the same?
4. What untapped potential might this relationship have for both of us?

Chances are, many of your relationships have a treasure trove of possibilities you haven't explored. That's an exciting discovery because it means there's space for the relationship to evolve and deepen. Imagine what your life can be like if you develop all your healthy relationships to their full potential.

Solidify Your Connections
Over time, you can strengthen *all* your connections, but start with just two. Choose two relationships you want to solidify, and create a one-year plan to make it happen. You can:

- Invite them to do more things more often, whether it's taking a coffee break, going for a walk or anything else you'll both enjoy.
- Be fully present when you're with them.
- Steer the conversation toward sharing experiences you've each had.
- Practice the good listening behaviors from Chapter Five. Remember that your goal is to understand what you're being told, not to try to fix it unless they ask for that type of support. My client Rose's boyfriend asks, "Is this a fix-it moment or a hug moment?" How great is that?
- Do things that you know the person will appreciate. It can be following up with a call or a text about

something they told you, giving them something they
mentioned that they wanted or needed or forwarding
them an article they'll find interesting or a playlist
they might like. My sister, Roberta, is great at this. She
never forgets a special occasion and always chooses
gifts she knows we'll love, like the chocolate-covered
fruit she sends my mom and me for our birthdays
every year. We all appreciate it when people think
of us and do something to show they value our
relationship. Everyone likes to be valued and feel
special.

- Write down the dates and details of important
  upcoming events they've told you about, and check
  in to see how things went. This can be as simple as
  a voice mail or a text message saying, "Hey, how did
  the doctor's appointment go today?" or "How did
  your presentation go?" or "Did your kids enjoy their
  recital?" Showing people that you're paying attention
  to what's going on in their lives and that you care is an
  effective way to ensure that they know they're being
  seen, heard, and valued.

Develop Deeper Connections

If you want to develop deeper, more meaningful connections,
begin building those bridges with your own vulnerability:

- Dive deeper. When you're talking to someone, leave
  the superficial behind. Instead of talking about the
  weather or the day's news, ask about their parents,
  their significant other or their children. And be willing
  to let down your guard and share something similar
  that's challenging for you. Deepening the conversation

isn't just sharing information—it's talking about the *significance* of an event. If your father had a stroke, you don't stop with stating the fact. You share something about the effect it had on you: "My father had a stroke, and seeing him that way made me realize he's not invincible. It really shook me up."

- Make a pact with yourself to be honest. Don't lie about your past—including embarrassing things you might have said or done—and don't embellish or exaggerate the lackluster moments to make them look better. Owning everything about your past makes you stronger, more approachable and more relatable. Being able to admit that you've been wrong and that you've failed will help you develop deeper connections.

EXPAND YOUR VILLAGE

When Lara left the CEO position in India and founded Work Coherence, she was showered with encouragement from her personal board of directors and hundreds of people in the villages she'd built around the world. In every company and country where she worked she met new people and saw potential in them even when they didn't see it themselves. Many people succeeded because of the opportunities she gave them and the mentoring and guidance she provided. So they wanted her to succeed and immediately began referring clients and offering other types of support. "It was amazing," she says. "They were so excited about what I was doing. They want everyone to lead a coherent life with purpose as much as I do."

To expand your village, when you engage with new people notice what makes them unique and consider how you might help each other. Do you have skills, talents, perspectives or experience that can improve each other's villages? Never underestimate the influence your actions and words can have. You can be the mentor or guide who offers a hand up when someone needs it the most. You can be that "someone" who makes all the difference for somebody else or for many people. An easy way to begin the expansion is to choose two people you want to add to your village and commit to developing relationships with them over the next year. Choose one person who will be a great addition because they have values, hobbies or interests similar to yours and you can learn a lot from them. This person will be someone you're acquainted with, admire, and want to develop a closer relationship with. And choose another person who can benefit by having you in *their* village. It might be a family member, an old friend you've lost touch with, an elder who needs support or companionship or someone you can mentor.

Your objective is to invest in these relationships and grow them to their full potential. By doing this, you'll enrich their lives as well as your own. We can't give something without receiving something in the process, even if that "something" is the simple pleasure of knowing we helped. Scientific researchers have learned that altruism activates reward centers in the brain that are associated with pleasure, so receiving is part of giving!

We've all experienced the joy of selfless giving, but two of my clients showed me just how extraordinary the benefits can be. During my internship, I worked at one of the largest counseling centers in Alberta, where clients were charged a sliding fee based on what they could afford. The people I counseled had struggles as diverse as their backgrounds, and I got to see just how important mental health is. While I worked there, I became a big believer that counseling should be available to everyone, so when I opened my private practice, I allocated a number of sessions each week to see clients at a discounted rate. Several clients I'd worked with during my internship called to ask about my private practice fees, and while I wasn't able to extend the same discount they'd received at the big center, I *was* able to offer them an affordable fee that was a small fraction of my rate.

If it sounds like I'm being altruistic, it's because I've only told you half the story.

Initially, I thought of it as altruism too. It was my way of contributing and walking my talk that therapy should be affordable for everyone. But it's become clear that I'm learning as much from them as they're learning from me, and at the end of some sessions, I've learned so much and been so inspired that there's no doubt I'm getting the better part of the bargain. These clients have done such great work to transform their lives that they inspire me to be a better person. They've shown me how far humans can go. They've shown me how much change is possible. They've shown me that despite the past, the future can always be bright, that the future always has possibilities. And for that I'm eternally grateful to them.

As you develop your own relationships, you'll see that the roles of giver and receiver often flip-flop. The person you committed to helping may end up helping you in unexpected ways, and you may end up being the one who gains the most from the experience. Meanwhile, the person you're striving to emulate may end up learning something valuable from you. So be sure you're not locking yourself or other people into just one side of the equation. You can be a giver and a receiver, a teacher and a student, a leader and a servant—all within the same relationship.

IN BRIEF

- Whether you call it a board of directors, dream team or village, research studies and empirical evidence make a powerful case for actively developing relationships with people who want to help you to succeed.
- Fostering trust and authenticity isn't a "soft" skill—it's an essential element of a company's success.
- Your village will expand your potential with their knowledge and experience *and* encourage you to take calculated risks for the sake of following your dreams and making the impact you want to make.
- Ideally, you'll build a village with about fifteen people, and a handful of them will be like a village council.
- Not every relationship can be remodeled or repaired. Sometimes disconnecting is the only healthy choice.
- You can make your village stronger by including people with a variety of strengths and talents and diverse backgrounds and beliefs. It can also be particularly helpful to include people who disagree with you.
- Fortifying your village means taking the initiative to strengthen your connections and show people how

valuable they are to you. This includes being proactive about maintaining these relationships, often over time and across long distances.

- Chances are, many of your relationships have a treasure trove of possibilities you haven't explored. That's an exciting discovery because it means there's space for the relationships to evolve and deepen.
- You can be a giver and a receiver, a teacher and a student, a leader and a servant—all within the same relationship.

———

In Chapter Eight, we'll look at what makes people most compatible, including core beliefs, attunement, and attachment styles.

CHAPTER 8

NAVIGATE COMPATIBILITY DIFFERENCES

When my client Beth was scrolling through her Instagram feed and saw a photo of her friend Janice with a former co-worker she couldn't stand, she was stunned. "I knew Janice was going to Patagonia with a few friends, but I didn't know Tiffany was one of them," she said. "I didn't even know they knew each other."

It turned out that Janice and Tiffany had met when they volunteered at a nature preserve in Costa Rica, and when they found out about the eco-conservation efforts in Patagonia, they decided to go together.

"Janice is one of the kindest people I know," Beth said, "and Tiffany is one of the rudest. How can they be friends?"

"Did Janice tell you what she likes about Tiffany?" I asked.

"That's the craziest part. The person Janice described didn't sound anything like the Tiffany I knew."

Beth and I had been talking about the components that make people compatible, so I asked her what she and Janice had in common.

"We're definitely in sync about a lot of things. Family is

really important to both of us, and we're both vegetarians and into the whole sustainable lifestyle thing." She said they also had similar styles of connecting and were attuned to each other's feelings.

Having values in common and similar styles of connecting supports strong relationships, and so does attunement. But we hadn't explored the other big one: core beliefs—the deeply held truths we have about ourselves and others that are integral to how we see the world.

"Do you think of life as an adventure or more like something to survive?" I said.

She laughed. "So far my whole life's been about surviving. Hasn't been much time for adventures. At least not fun ones."

"How about Janice? Is that true for her too?"

"Not at all," she said. "Janice always thinks things will work out for her, and somehow they usually do."

Hearing her describe Janice made me think of my sister, Roberta, who sees the glass as half full and has a super-positive worldview. "What about Tiffany?" I said. "Is that how she thinks too?"

She looked up at the ceiling like she was trying to remember. "Actually, I think it might be. When we set project goals, she was always pushing us to go higher and saying things like 'Just trust the universe,' and I was worried that she wasn't considering all the risks."

Beth had a core belief that the world isn't inherently good; it's a place to survive. This informed her worldview that people are dangerous and can't always be trusted and that it's reasonable to be fearful because bad things happen. Her friend Janice had a core belief that the world *is* inherently good; it's a place to thrive. This informed her worldview that people can be trusted and that there's no reason to be fearful—things have a way of working out.

Because Beth's and Tiffany's core beliefs were fundamentally different, they had a hard time getting along. But having *similar* core beliefs is one of the things that can help people to click, and Janice and Tiffany got along great because they were both adventurous, considered the world a safe place to explore and had an easy time trusting people. Beth was envious of their connection, but she wasn't interested in joining them. From her perspective, there were real dangers that Janice didn't take into account, and she wasn't comfortable putting herself in what she considers risky situations.

Since our core beliefs form the foundation of our point of view, neither Beth nor Janice is right or wrong. They just see things differently. Their friendship had endured many years, so the difference in their core beliefs wasn't a deal-breaker for them, and it doesn't have to be for anyone else. The key is to build and develop relationships based on the components we *do* have in common and learn how to respectfully navigate the differences.

Compatibility Components

There are a number of components that can enhance our compatibility in a relationship. The top three are core beliefs, attunement, and attachment styles. While having some or all of these components in common can make relationships easier, it's often the differences that make relationships interesting.

- **Core Beliefs:** Core beliefs are integral to the way you see the world—your worldview. These deeply embedded "truths" determine how you experience reality. Core beliefs guide your choices and behavior and strongly influence how you perceive yourself, others, and every aspect of life.

- **Attunement:** Attunement is the ability to emotionally "see" someone.
- **Attachment Styles:** Formed in childhood, attachment styles reflect the way you were loved in your first years of life and affect all your adult relationships.

When we get along easily with someone, it's often because some of our compatibility components are aligned. When we don't get along with someone, if we can figure out which components aren't compatible, we can often find a middle ground.

DO YOU SEE THE WORLD THE SAME WAY?

Once Beth realized that Janice and Tiffany had similar core beliefs, including the way they see the world, she could understand why they were friends. So instead of being envious, she decided to deepen her own relationship with Janice and invited her family to the vacation house they'd rented.

On the first day of the visit, "the guys" went fishing and Beth and Janice had the day to reminisce and catch up. It was exactly the kind of bonding Beth was hoping for, and when they said good night, she felt like they hadn't missed a beat since college.

The next day while their husbands were playing golf, Beth and Janice took their ten-year-old sons into town, but after stopping in a few shops it was clear that their idea of a good time wasn't the same as the boys'. "Let's let them roam," Janice said. "What can happen in Lake Placid?"

Beth wasn't a helicopter mom, but she liked to know where Todd was and what he was doing. She believed that kids need a certain amount of supervision and guidance and that it was her job to provide that. Meanwhile, Janice believed kids should be given a lot of freedom to explore. In short, Beth and Janice had been raised differently, and each was raising her son the way *she'd* been raised. After a few tense moments of negotiating, they met each other halfway by giving the boys permission to explore, but only on Main Street, and they had to meet back at the bookstore in an hour.

When Beth told me this story, she said she was a nervous wreck the entire time. She'd never let her son roam without adult supervision, and she wasn't so naïve to believe that bad things didn't happen in small towns. That night, Beth told Janice how she'd felt. "I know it's a small town, but kids can get in trouble anywhere," she said.

"Getting in trouble is how kids learn," Janice said.

"True, but some mistakes can't be undone, like getting hit by a car."

Janice laughed. "Nobody was going more than five miles an hour."

Beth knew she should change the subject, but getting laughed at made her press her point. "Fine. But other bad things could have happened. Just last week a boy Todd's age was almost kidnapped on the way to school—in a very safe neighborhood."

"Oh my God, you've been watching too much news," Janice said. "Bad things happen all the time. You can let fear run *your* life, but I'm not going to let it run mine."

Clearly, they weren't going to agree about the right way to raise kids, so they changed the subject and later decided that the next time they got together, it would be just the two of them.

When a relationship hits a bump in the road, sometimes

you can smooth the way just by finding out what's beneath the bump. If you discover that you and your friend have conflicting views about parenting, you can renovate your relationship so that the kids aren't involved. If you have a co-worker who rubs you the wrong way, you can make a sincere effort to discover the underlying factors. Do you have clashing worldviews? Do you feel disregarded or "unseen" when you interact with them? You can't improve a relationship if you don't determine the root of the problem and try to understand the other person's point of view. When we make a sincere attempt to understand, it changes how we see people and makes it easier to separate the actions or behavior we don't like from the individual. Beth didn't really hate Tiffany—she just hated the way she felt when Tiffany pushed for goals that were outside her own comfort zone.

Core beliefs are ideas we tend to think of as "right" and "true," so they frame the way we interpret situations, circumstances and other people's actions. What's important to keep in mind is that core beliefs aren't actually right or wrong. We can improve relationships with people who have different core beliefs when we understand that their "truths" were formed by their upbringing and experiences, just as ours were.

If you're having a hard time accepting someone's core beliefs, consider what yours might be if you'd been born into their family and walked in their shoes. What's considered good and right in a certain place at a certain time can be considered bad and wrong in other circumstances. For example:

- Beliefs and norms about marriage and divorce differ around the world. In some places, teens are encouraged to date and have sex before they get married to prepare them to choose a good mate.

In other places, marriages are arranged, brides are expected to be virgins and divorce isn't an option. The core belief in these societies is that marriage lasts forever and people have to make it work or suffer the consequences. In other societies, if marriage doesn't contribute to your happiness, it's perfectly acceptable to end the union and move on.

- In some places, including North America, once kids are adults, they're expected to move out of their parents' home and get a place of their own. In other places, including Latin America, kids often live with their parents well into their twenties or until they get married.

- If you believe in asceticism, you live simply and practice abstinence. But if you embrace the western value that you only live once—YOLO—you want to get the most out of life.

Since our core beliefs were developed when we were children, it's not unusual to grow up believing they were true without questioning them. But when we're adults, these beliefs have so much power over our perceptions that they can hinder our ability to form happy, healthy relationships. So it's important to explore and question your hard "truths" from time to time to see if they're limiting you from having better relationships or a more fulfilling life.

Albert Einstein said, "The most important decision we make is whether we believe we live in a friendly or hostile universe." Imagine that people who believe the world is friendly are wearing gold-lens glasses and people who believe the world is hostile are wearing glasses with gray lenses. Now imagine that each group has been wearing their glasses every day since they were about three years old. Naturally, the way they see the world is their reality. Worldview works a lot like those glasses, filtering and coloring everything we observe and experience. If you're wearing the golden glasses, you see all the possibilities, the beauty and the blessings amid or embedded in your experiences. If you're wearing the gray glasses, you see dangers, risks, and challenges everywhere.

I got to experience the effects of these polar opposites when I went on a three-week tour of India's golden triangle with my friend Lucimar. There were about a dozen people in our tour group, and one of them turned out to be one of my friend's mom, who I met for the first time while we were waiting to board our flight. "It's all so wonderful," Sonia said, smiling from ear to ear, as we talked about the places we were going to visit. It *was* wonderful and I was excited to visit India for the first time with my good friend, but as we lined up to board, I couldn't help noticing that the couple behind us didn't look happy at all. As Sonia and a friend talked about what an incredible opportunity this trip was and how exciting it was to be going on an adventure in a country they'd never visited before, you'd never have known that the couple behind us was headed for the same destination. I'll call them Bill and Karen, and they were complaining about how long the flight was going to be, worrying whether they'd be able to digest Indian food and arguing about which foods were safe to eat. Suddenly, I was worrying too. But not about Indian food or the flight.

Please don't let my seat be next to theirs.

Fortunately, that prayer was answered, and twenty-some hours later, after two flights and a long layover, we landed in New Delhi—where, to my surprise, I found myself starting to appreciate where Bill and Karen were coming from with all their concerns. As ready as I'd been to get off that plane, I wasn't prepared for the wall-to-wall people in the airport. I'd never seen so many people packed so close together in my entire life. I later learned that Indira Gandhi International Airport is the busiest airport in Asia and at the time the second-busiest in the world. It was modern and air-conditioned, but that didn't quell the wave of claustrophobia that was washing over me. And the sudden onslaught of unfamiliar sights, sounds, and smells wasn't helping.

I had to stand still for a moment, close my eyes and go to my internal happy place. After a few long, slow breaths, I calmed down enough to wade into the river of people and let it carry me to baggage claim, which *had* to be less crowded. As it turned out, though, there were so many people between the carousel and me that I watched my orange suitcase go by twice before I was able to wriggle my way in close enough to grab it.

Finally, with bag in hand, I went outside and joined the people from our group who were waiting to board the bus that would take us to the hotel. It was so hot that it took a minute to catch my breath.

Just breathe . . . How can anybody survive this heat? I thought. "It's all so wonderful."

I turned to see Sonia smiling behind me, and I was reminded that I was on this trip to see and experience new things, and that's exactly what was happening.

And it continued to happen on the bus ride, which was a trip in itself. Hundreds of drivers were blowing their horns at the same time, and if there were traffic laws, nobody was obeying them. So many horns were blaring that I could barely hear what Lucimar was saying even though the bus windows were closed and she was sitting right next to me. It was a wonder anyone managed to get anywhere, but we eventually made it to the hotel in one piece.

The next day when Lucimar and I went to the hotel's dining room for breakfast, Sonia was already there and her smile was just as big and bright as it had been at the airport. "Good morning!" she said as she dipped a *dosa*—a crepe made of lentils—into a bowl of chutney. "It's all so wonderful." I had to laugh to myself as, a few tables away, Bill and Karen shared a can of tomato juice and tried to decide if anything on the menu was safe to eat.

Over the next few days, I noticed that whether we were doing something as remarkable as touring the Taj Mahal or something as everyday as eating sun-ripened mangoes, Sonia's pleasant demeanor was the same. For her, both the palace and the mango were "so wonderful." And her attitude proved contagious. Before long, I found myself saying, "It's all so wonderful," too.

Meanwhile, Bill and Karen complained about how much walking we had to do at the palace and how much their feet hurt. They didn't try the mangoes even though the fruit's protective skin was perfectly intact, because mangoes weren't on their list of safe foods. I couldn't help wondering why they came to India. Were they like this all the time, or was the trip bringing out the worst in them?

One day after touring the Hawa Mahal palace, our bus was taking us back to the hotel for a relaxing afternoon, but Sonia, Lucimar, and I wanted to visit the jewelry stores because emeralds and sapphires are a lot less expensive in India than they are at home. So in the middle of a busy intersection in the center of Jaipur, we left the comfort of the air-conditioned bus and braved the scorching heat and blaring horns and managed to make our way to the side of the road without being run over. We weaved our way through the crowd and visited dozens of stores before each of us had found what we had our hearts set on and haggled with the jewelers until we were satisfied with the prices. "It's all so wonderful," Sonia said as we headed outside in victory.

By then it was already dark and we hadn't eaten anything since breakfast. None of us could speak or read the local languages, so we didn't know what the menus posted outside the restaurants said or what the food vendors were saying. Even if they spoke English, their accents were too thick for us to understand. Covered in street dust and on the verge of fainting from hunger, we finally spotted a stand selling bananas, bought two big bunches and ate every single one of them. When we were done, we were so giddy that we were all laughing helplessly and saying, "It's all so wonderful," even though we had no idea where we were or how we were getting back to the hotel.

We eventually figured out that the only way back was to hire a *tuk-tuk*, which is a motorized rickshaw, and as we boarded one laughing and wearing "golden glasses," I handed the driver a slip of paper with the hotel name and address. He nodded and said something in Hindi and we were off. It was a long bumpy ride, and all the while we were wondering if he was taking us to the right place. It didn't matter, though—we were riding high on the "It's all so wonderful" vibe. When we finally pulled up in front of our fancy hotel right alongside a Rolls-Royce and a Lamborghini, the valet came running over with his mouth hanging open, and we started laughing all over again. Apparently, nobody had ever arrived at the Oberoi Raj Vilas in a *tuk-tuk*.

When Bill and Karen spotted us in the lobby, they greeted us as if we'd been missing for days. It was sweet that they were sincerely worried about us, and it was also another example of how worldview determines how safe or unsafe we feel in various situations. While they'd been at the hotel talking about how they'd probably never see us again, we were having the time of our lives. What could have been a scary experience and a low point of the trip had turned into one of the most fun and memorable days, almost entirely because Sonia's spirit of optimism was like a wave, lifting us up and propelling us forward. It's been years since that trip, but every time I wear my sapphire necklace, the memories come rushing back along with the smiles. It's a heartwarming reminder that, yes, it *is* all so wonderful.

Relationships with people who share your worldview can be easier to develop and smoother to navigate because you see life in a similar way. That's true whether you're wearing the golden glasses or the gray ones. Relationships with people who see the world through different lenses can take the most work to develop, but it's worth the effort. If your tendency is to see the world as hostile, having people in your village who see it as friendly and inviting can help you to shift your view toward the positive. On the other hand, if you typically see the world as safe and friendly, villagers who see the world as dangerous are always assessing the risks and working on contingency plans. Both views are valuable.

ARE YOU IN TUNE WITH EACH OTHER'S FEELINGS?

When we're emotionally attuned to someone, we recognize, understand and are able to empathize with what they're experiencing. This is an important part of all good relationships, but it's particularly important with friends, people we work closely with, and romantic partners. If we feel like someone doesn't "see" us, it's impossible to develop a healthy relationship with them, and the same is true for others when *we* don't see *them*.

Attunement is an essential component for creating deeper connection and intimacy. While you may have a friend or partner who understands you so well that you rarely have to explain how you're feeling, not everyone has this ability, and some have to work hard to develop it. Attunement isn't something we can take for granted—it's possible to love someone but not be attuned with them. If we value a relationship, it's on us to frequently ask how the other person is doing and follow up to see if their words are aligned with their feelings. In some ways, attunement is intangible—we pick up a vibe or somehow just know someone's not feeling quite right—but whether this comes naturally to you or not, you can develop your ability to attune to others by paying close attention to them and noticing how what you say and do affects them.

Being able to attune to others isn't just necessary for friendships and partnerships—it's also important in the workplace. If you're working with people you don't have attunement with, every day can be challenging, especially if:

- You're dealing with difficult problems in your personal life, such as divorce, a family member's death or illness, or issues with your children.
- You have special needs.
- There's someone in your life with special needs, such as a parent with dementia or a child with a neurological or physical difference.

The more challenges you face in your personal life, the more support and understanding you need from your co-workers.

When they're attuned to you, they'll get why you disappeared in the middle of the day and be more flexible about making concessions. When they're not attuned to you, life can become a lot harder very quickly, especially when the person who's out of attunement is your boss. My client Robyn found herself in this situation a few months after she learned her son was autistic. She'd negotiated a flexible work schedule so she could be responsive to Ryan's needs, but every time she left the office early or came in late, her boss made snide comments like "Had enough work for one day, have you?" or "How nice of you to come in." Adding insult to injury, Deborah was constantly bragging about how awesome her twins were doing and utterly clueless about how it sounded to Robyn, who was still reeling from Ryan's diagnosis.

Robyn was coming to therapy to work through her grief and her anxiety about Ryan's future, and now that Deborah was pushing back about their flex-time agreement, her anxiety was sky-high. Over the next several months, Robyn's respect for Deborah deteriorated because she bragged about her high-achieving twins on an almost-daily basis and never once asked how Ryan was doing.

"She's so self-absorbed and enchanted with her own kids that I don't even know if she remembers Ryan's autistic," Robyn said. "The other day I was in the lunchroom telling one of my co-workers about Ryan working with a therapist to practice regulating his emotions so he has fewer meltdowns. At some point Deborah showed up and stood next to the table until I finished talking. And then, instead of commenting on what I'd said, she bragged about her eight-year-olds being accepted in some junior genius program. What a narcissist."

As Robyn and I worked through her frustration with her boss, she realized that Deborah wasn't actually doing anything *to* her. She was just a proud parent bragging about her incredibly bright kids. "I know she's not trying to make me feel bad," Robyn said, "but how can the mother of such smart kids be so emotionally out of touch that she doesn't even think about how it's affecting me?"

Over time, Robyn learned to stop taking Deborah's behavior personally and turned her attention to herself and how *she* might sometimes be out of touch with how other people are feeling, especially when she felt overwhelmed. The dynamic with Deborah motivated her to become much more cognizant of the power of her own words and actions. "I kind of hate to admit it," she said," but because of Deborah, I make it a point to tune in to what other people are feeling before I share anything myself, and I always think about how my words might affect other people before I say them."

Robyn could have continued feeling victimized by her boss, but instead she chose to use Deborah's lack of attunement as an opportunity to grow and become a better person herself.

DO YOU CONNECT THE SAME WAY?

Our self-worth and ability to trust others significantly influence the way we relate to partners, family members, friends, and co-workers. Since the foundations of trust and self-worth are laid in childhood, the way adults like to connect with other adults has a lot to do with how we were raised. Research shows that about 50 percent of adults feel secure about connecting with other people, and if you're in this group, you probably had primary caregivers who were responsive to your needs and provided you with a sense of security. If you're not in this group, close or intimate relationships may make you feel anxious or afraid, or you may avoid them altogether. As with people in the "secure" group, your style of attaching to others was also strongly influenced by your upbringing. But unlike the people in that group, your "attachment style" may be limiting your relationships.

Your attachment style affects your ability to honestly communicate your needs and desires, your attitudes toward sex and other intimate topics, the way you handle conflict, and your view of togetherness and intimacy. Research on adult attachment styles has repeatedly confirmed that there are four primary styles across a wide range of cultures and countries. The four styles are:

1. Secure
2. Anxious
3. Avoidant
4. Anxious/Avoidant

Relationship dynamics are largely driven by the attachment styles of the people involved, so if you're having difficulty, consider whether it's because the two of you connect in different ways. The following descriptions can help you identify your attachment style and the styles of the people you interact with.

Secure Attachment Style

About 50 percent of adults worldwide have a secure attachment style.

People with a secure attachment style are comfortable expressing emotions, trust their close friends and partner and feel safe being emotionally and physically intimate. They enjoy close relationships but don't depend on their partners' or friends' approval, because they already feel worthy. If your attachment style is secure, you can probably speak up for yourself and aren't threatened by opinions that differ from or conflict with your own. If at first you don't succeed, even if you wipe out spectacularly, you can get up and keep moving forward without being broken by the experience. When two people with secure attachment styles are in a relationship, they can be themselves and depend on each other. These relationships are built with honesty, acceptance, and emotional connection.

Anxious Attachment Style

About 20 percent of the adult population worldwide has anxious attachment style.

People with an anxious attachment style tend to have a positive view of their partners and friends but a negative view of themselves. They often see the other people in their relationships as their "better halves" and may worry that they'll leave them or end the friendship. Because they're afraid of being rejected and abandoned, they can become needy and clingy, adding strain to the relationship and often testing its limits. People with this attachment style crave intimacy, but no matter how much love their partner and friends give them, it's never quite enough to fill the void created in their childhood. Their upbringing has predisposed them to being distrustful, suspicious, and quick to feel offended.

Avoidant Attachment Style

About 25 percent of the adult population worldwide has avoidant attachment style.

People with avoidant attachment style struggle to establish close friendships and intimate relationships because they conflict with their need for independence and autonomy. While these lone wolves tend to like themselves and have high self-esteem, they're often locked in an internal battle between craving closeness and avoiding it. They're afraid of intimacy because they didn't see it or experience it when they were kids. Consequently, they like being emotionally strong and self-sufficient, don't like to depend on others and don't want other people to depend on them. They aren't especially interested in what others think of them and rarely ask for help. To avoid feeling vulnerable, they hide their feelings and steer clear of commitments even though a loving connection is often what they want most. Since strong and close relationships contribute to longer, happier lives, it's a good idea for people with avoidant style to work toward becoming more comfortable with closeness and intimacy.

Anxious/Avoidant Attachment Style

About 5 percent of the adult population worldwide has anxious/avoidant attachment style.

People with a style that's a combination of anxious and avoidant want close and intimate relationships, but because they have a hard time trusting others, creating that closeness can be very difficult. They want to love and be loved, but they're afraid of intimacy and vulnerability, so they tend to avoid close relationships to protect themselves from being disappointed or hurt. People with this attachment style were often raised by caregivers who were unable to provide the comfort and soothing they needed. Instead of being a secure base, the caregivers were a source of distress. In these families, typically one or both parents exhibited unstable behavior ranging from being unavailable, anxious, or uncertain when their child needed them, to being emotionally or physically abusive.

Attachment Style Combinations

When people's attachment styles are compatible, relationships can be relatively easy to create and develop. When they're not compatible, they can still be satisfying if you're both willing to do a little work.

Secure Style with Anxious Style or Avoidant Style

People with secure attachment style can navigate relationships with people who have anxious or avoidant styles, but it takes more work than developing a relationship with someone who also has a secure style.

People with a secure style want close relationships, but people with avoidant style don't allow themselves to get too involved. This behavior is usually driven by fear of rejection or abandonment. When someone with an avoidant style realizes they're feeling closer to someone, they're more likely to pull back or disconnect than to risk intimacy.

People with anxious style also fear being rejected and abandoned, but instead of pulling back, their fear motivates them to be clingy and need constant validation and reassurance.

Anxious Style with Avoidant Style

If one person has anxious style and the other has avoidant style, they have opposing needs.

The anxious needs closeness and intimacy and pushes for these needs to be addressed, but the avoidant feels overwhelmed by these bids and tends to withdraw even more. When the avoidant pulls back, the anxious becomes overwhelmed. As a result, their fear of being abandoned is triggered, so they try even harder to get closer to their avoidant partner or friend. This perpetuates a negative cycle, with each person's actions resulting in the opposite of what they're trying to achieve.

For this relationship to work, both people need to learn to interpret each other's actions as a consequence of their attachment style. They can also practice not taking the other's actions personally and being less reactive.

Anxious Style with Anxious Style

If both people in a relationship have anxious attachment style, they both want closeness and intimacy, so they may feel like they've finally found a kindred spirit, or "the one," and become attached very quickly. In romantic relationships the bliss is hard to miss, but it can also be hard to sustain because people with anxious style have a hard time managing the jealousy they feel when their partner shows interest in other people or even hobbies or pastimes. If this romantic combination were in a movie, they'd have explosive arguments followed by atomic make-up sex.

Avoidant Style with Avoidant Style

Two people with avoidant style are willing to discuss any topic in depth except their emotions and personal needs. Whether they're friends or partners, they usually have friends who aren't mutual and have a variety of separate interests or pastimes. A relationship between people with avoidant attachment style can work well because they both want autonomy and space and neither is especially demanding of the other. If they discover that they want more emotional closeness, they can work on learning to increase their trust levels and practice letting their guard down to develop deeper emotional bonds over time.

Anxious and Avoidant Style with Anxious and Avoidant Style

There are a variety of style combinations among people with anxious and avoidant styles, and they each have unique challenges because the people involved oscillate between being anxious and avoidant in different situations and circumstances. This can make for a wild ride, but the twists and turns can become easier to navigate if both people are willing to work on themselves and invest in the relationship's success.

To navigate this combination, the person with the more secure attachment style can increase their understanding of how people with anxious or avoidant styles think and feel about relationships. Learning how they were raised can give you helpful insights into their behavior and stop you from taking it personally.

If your style is anxious:

- Identify your fearful thoughts about rejection and abandonment so you can start to change undesirable attachment-related behaviors.
- Tell your partner that you sometimes have a bigger need to be reassured, acknowledged, or loved.

If your style is avoidant:

- Identify your fears about intimacy, connection, and vulnerability and work on withdrawing less when your partner, friends or family members have emotional needs.

- Communicate honestly. Tell them when you feel overwhelmed and ask for a few hours or a day to regulate your emotions before you come back to the discussion or address their needs.

Understanding how attachment styles affect your interactions can be helpful for all your relationships, but no matter what style you use, you can gravitate toward a more secure style by becoming more self-aware and working on self-improvement. This will help you to reduce the frequency and intensity of behaviors that can strain relationships. People who don't have secure attachment styles can also become more secure when they're in relationships with those who do.

While attachment styles, attunement and core beliefs all affect our relationships, if we commit to finding common ground and learn to navigate our differences, we can develop a relationship with just about anyone.

IN BRIEF

- Core beliefs are ideas you tend to think of as "right" and "true," and they determine how you see yourself, others and the world. They frame the way you interpret situations, circumstances, and other people's actions.
- Attunement is the ability to emotionally "see" someone.

- Attachment styles reflect the way you were loved in your first years of life and affect all your adult relationships.
- Relationships with people who share your worldview can be easier to develop and smoother to navigate because you view life in a similar way.
- Attunement is an essential component for creating deeper connection and intimacy. Much like empathy, it's about being in tune with another person's emotions.
- Your self-worth and ability to trust others significantly influence the way you relate to partners and close friends.
- Your attachment style affects your ability to honestly communicate your needs and desires, your attitudes toward sex, the way you handle conflict and your view of togetherness and intimacy.
- No matter what attachment style you have, you can develop a more secure style by becoming more self-aware, communicating your needs and working with a therapist to bridge the divide between what your heart yearns for and the fear or anxiety that gets in the way.

In Chapter Nine, we'll look at how making a lasting impact can fulfill your purpose and feed the wheel of good.

CHAPTER 9

MAKE A LASTING IMPACT

"Everyone has their own purpose," says Brad Aronson, angel investor, teacher, and author of *HumanKind: Changing the World One Small Act At a Time*. "For me, it's being helpful and trying to make life better for other people. For someone else, it could be coding because that's what they love doing."

Brad measures his success by how much his life lines up with his purpose. "When I'm doing what I believe I'm meant to be doing and having fun, I know I'm aligned with my purpose. That means being a good husband, a good father, a good family member, a good friend and a good community member." But he's quick to point out that depending on circumstances, not everyone is able to pursue their purpose as soon as they know what it is. "For some people, following their purpose might be something they do outside of work because they have responsibilities or burdens that limit their options, at least temporarily."

Ideally, we can all eventually find a way to pursue our purpose and be financially secure, and Brad is committed to helping young people make that happen. He teaches entrepreneurship to young adults through the nonprofit Hopeworks in

Philadelphia, Pennsylvania and Camden, New Jersey. The organization uses education, technology, and entrepreneurship to help young people succeed in life, and in addition to teaching and mentoring, Brad has served on the board. He's also an active supporter of Big Brothers Big Sisters. "I love teaching and helping young people to see opportunities and encouraging them," he says. "Seeing amazing young people working hard and reaching their potential inspires me."

Brad is living his *ikigai*—he's doing what he loves, what he's good at, and what the world needs. And while he doesn't receive financial compensation for his teaching, he says, "The rewards are much greater than any dollar amount could be." That's been a theme in Brad's life all along. When he graduated from college, his first job was as a live-in tutor at a group home for academically gifted inner-city kids. When he accepted the job, many people said things like, "After spending all that money on college, shouldn't you be doing something else?"

"I didn't care what anyone thought about it," he says. "I was so excited and so happy. I loved that job. I think it might still be my favorite job. And it's a perfect example of doing what I wanted to do even though it didn't align with other people's definition of success."

The idea of doing what we're excited about is something Brad tries to pass on to the young adults he teaches. "I think a huge challenge for people is differentiating between their personal metrics of success and what they think they *should* be doing. I encourage the students to set goals that really hit home for them instead of shooting for what they've been told is appropriate."

MAKING A LASTING IMPACT TAKES COURAGE

Knowing our *ikigai*, or purpose, is one thing. Living it is another. Pursuing what we're passionate about often requires courage, and so does living according to our individual values—especially when they don't align with society's definition of success or our family's. Once again, this is where the freedom to choose comes into play. We can choose to live as survivors, doing what it takes to get by, or we can choose to live with intention, doing what's most meaningful. Living with purpose usually isn't the easiest path, but scientific studies and life experience show that it's the healthiest, most fulfilling path.

When Brad started a digital ad agency a few years after graduating from college, there was no shortage of people to question his choice. In 1996, internet marketing was new, many companies didn't even have a website and the company websites that existed were very basic. "I thought the internet was the best marketing venue I'd ever seen," Brad says, "so I started i-frontier to help companies use online marketing." Because the internet and everything about it was a new frontier, many of the people who heard Brad's plan thought he'd be better off getting a job with an established company. Fortunately, his family and close friends supported his choice, and his wife, Mia, not only believed in him but took on an extra job when the growing company was short on money.

There are many obstacles to following our own path, including resistance from others, so having a village that believes in our vision and is willing to help us achieve it is imperative. A strong, connected village will help you over obstacles, encourage you when the learning curve is steep and support the changes you're making. Change can be scary, but when your village has your back, it's a little easier to take a chance. As the eighteenth century physicist Georg C. Lichtenberg said, "I cannot say whether things will get better if we change; what I can say is they must change if they are to get better."

If we allow fear to stop us, whether it's fear of failure, rejection, judgment or anything else, we forfeit the freedom to make the impact we want to make. The next time you think, *What if I fail?*, challenge yourself with the question "What if I fly?" If you don't take the risks that can lead to a happier, more meaningful life, you may be settling for a limited, unhappy existence. If you make the changes that are aligned with your purpose or values, you give yourself the opportunity to grow wings.

Examples of risky changes I see clients make in search of more meaningful lives:

- Changing careers
- Having a child. Or another one. Or a third . . .
- Reengaging with a favorite hobby
- Going back to school
- Investing in an initiative that's important to them
- Traveling
- Reinventing themselves
  - Focusing on the three health pillars: nutrition, exercise, sleep
  - Letting go of relationships that imprison them
  - Rekindling relationships with friends from long ago
  - Moving to a different house or location

Every change we make takes effort, and some are very challenging and even painful. But when we're clear about the difference we want to make and we're making changes to achieve that vision, suffering and hardships are more tolerable because we know our "why." In *Man's Search for Meaning*, Viktor Frankl says, "There is nothing in the world, I venture to say, that so effectively helps one to survive even the worse conditions as the knowledge that there is a meaning in one's life."[1] Finding meaning is important no matter what we're pursuing, but when we set the bar high, meaning is essential because we're bound to have uphill battles and we probably won't win them all. When my client Felicia had a heart attack in her early thirties, the road back to health looked long and daunting and she wasn't sure she was up for the task. Making matters worse, the three weeks she spent recovering gave her plenty of time to realize how much she disliked her job. "When I think about going back to work, I start to sweat and my heart races," she told me. "Unemployment checks won't be enough to get by. I already checked. But I don't think I can do all the stuff my doctor says I have to do if I have to keep the IT job."

Over the next few weeks, I helped Felicia clarify her values and purpose. During this time, she was also making the dietary changes her doctor recommended, exercising every day and learning to meditate. "I thought I was going to hate all of this," she said, "but the more I do it and read about all the health and longevity benefits, the more into it I am. The science that supports my doctor's advice is really interesting."

Reading and learning were two of Felicia's favorite pastimes, and as she learned how nutrition, exercise, and meditation support physical and mental health, she was fascinated. The more she learned, the more questions she had. But then one day she had an *answer*. "I figured it out!" she said at the beginning of our session. "I know what my purpose is." She was smiling triumphantly. "I'm going back to school to get a degree in nutrition. I'm so excited about it that I don't even mind keeping the same job while I get my degree. I know I can help other people with what I've been learning, and that's very meaningful to me."

Felicia didn't rule out finding a new job while she was getting her nutrition degree, but it became less urgent when she reframed the suffering as part of her path to living her purpose. Usually, I'm the one who shares research findings with clients, but in this case Felicia was the one to mention a study. "I saw a study in the *Journal of Psychosomatic Research* that said people who have direction and meaning in their lives aren't as burdened by stress and life events," she said. "The researchers followed more than 900 adults over ten years, and the ones who said they had meaning and direction in their life had less cumulative effects from stress."

By the time Felicia turned thirty-five, she had a new lifestyle and a healthy body and had learned how to manage her stress. Best of all, she loved being a nutritionist and was making plans to open a clinic. And none of that would have happened if she hadn't been courageous enough to make the necessary changes.

Lead with Your Vision and Values

As Brad and his team grew i-frontier, their values and vision for the company were in alignment. "Our focus was always on taking care of our staff and coming up with ways to better help our clients," he says. "My approach was to hire people smarter than me and get out of the way."

The approach worked. Just seven years after Brad founded i-frontier, it was acquired by aQuantive. He'd be staying on to manage it as a division within the larger company, and the Monday after the deal was signed, he took his staff off-site to announce the acquisition and answer their questions. Right after the meeting, his assistant made a beeline for him. "I think you should listen to your voice mail," she said.

"There were three messages, all from my grandfather," Brad says. "Popop said he bought a share of aQuantive as soon as the stock exchange opened and then called the chief financial officer to let him know he was a stockholder and needed to see the company's financials." The call had gone to voice mail, though, so Popop called other people on the financial staff, but none of them answered either, and nobody returned his calls. He was very concerned and asked Brad to call him immediately. "When I called, Popop said, 'How can a company get clients if they don't answer their phones at nine in the morning? How will you stay in business? Can you get out of the deal?' He also assured me he'd keep making calls until someone answered. What Popop didn't know was that the company is located in Washington state. He'd left my new bosses messages at 6 a.m. Pacific time."

Brad laughs as he tells this story. "If you have people like Popop looking out for you, you'll be fine."

Since surrounding yourself with people who want you to succeed improves your chances, you can give yourself an edge by building and maintaining strong relationships with people who share your desire to become a better person and live a more meaningful life. This will also save time. Instead of trying to get approval from people who aren't aligned with your goals or convince naysayers that your vision is achievable, you can focus on consistently and persistently moving toward your vision so you can bring it to fruition. And if you're leading a team, you'll want your teammates to be aligned with your vision and values. Effective leaders sell their vision and get everyone on board because they know they can achieve much more when everyone has a shared purpose and is working toward the same goal.

When Brad started i-frontier, he created a team that was as

inspired as he was about helping businesses to benefit from the new opportunities that digital marketing offered. After being acquired by aQuantive, he continued to lead his division with the same vision and values, and when Microsoft bought the company, he happily accepted the offer to be the senior director of advertiser-and-publisher solutions. After working a year and a half at Microsoft, he decided he wanted to spend more time teaching and volunteering, so he left the company and made the changes that enabled him to earn his income as an angel investor, investing in start-up companies—a role that's also aligned with his purpose to make the world better for others.

It Takes a Village to Leave a Legacy

In 2014, Brad was on top of the world. He and Mia were happily married, they had a healthy five-year-old son and Brad was doing what he loved every day. So when he heard Mia's doctor say, "Mia has leukemia," it felt like his world had suddenly spun out from under him. He held on to the arm of his chair and tried to take in what the doctor was saying.

Mia would need a month of inpatient chemotherapy, followed by nine months of intense outpatient chemo. And that would be followed by another year and a half of maintenance chemo.

"After the treatment schedule was laid out," Brad says, "social workers assured us that because Jack was so young, he wouldn't become anxious or even realize that Mia wasn't as involved as long as I did all the things she'd been doing and kept a positive attitude." He shakes his head. "I was determined to do it, but I had no idea how."

Fortunately, he didn't have to figure that out himself. The village he'd spent a lifetime building sprang into action.

His brother, Rob, and his wife, Tippi, found out what people undergoing inpatient chemotherapy need, bought every item on the list and dropped the massive care package off just before Mia was admitted.

A fellow board member at Big Brothers Big Sisters gave him a list of the work he was going to take over for Brad and asked what else he could do.

A friend of Mia's came to visit almost every week and brought lunch and all the supplies for a craft project.

Brad's cousin and her husband entertained Jack on many weekends and even offered to take him on vacation with their own four kids.

Another friend of Mia's emailed Brad to let him know she'd taken care of signing Jack up for Little League and would make sure Jack was on a team with someone who could provide rides to practices and games.

Brad's and Mia's parents stayed for weeks at a time, entertaining Jack, doing laundry and staying positive.

And they had a long list of friends who could pick up Jack after school when Brad was at the hospital or at chemotherapy with Mia.

"Not one person ever mentioned a single logistical challenge," Brad says. "They all told us how happy they were that we'd asked and that they could help."

The members of Brad's village rallied when he needed them the most. "They saw every crack in our armor and rushed in to fill it," he says. Looking back, it reminds him of the Japanese tradition of filling cracks in pottery with gold, making the object even more beautiful. "Even though Mia was sick, our lives were more beautiful because of the outpouring of support and love. Even in the darkest moments, we weren't really alone. And we know we never will be."

When a patient advocate suggested Brad, Mia and Jack start projects to give them purpose and something positive to focus on, Brad knew immediately what his would be. While Mia wrote in a journal every day and Jack diligently pursued the goal of playing wiffle ball two hundred days in a row, Brad wrote about the people who were doing so much for them: the friends, family members and total strangers who were getting them through the crisis, often with the smallest gestures. And he didn't stop there.

"I knew the world was *full* of people whose inspiring stories didn't make the news," he says, "so I looked for stories online and asked everyone I knew to send me stories about people who were making a difference in some way or another."

The project took on a life of its own, and Brad decided to include the stories in a book, along with information about how readers can get personally involved. *HumanKind: Changing the World One Small Act at a Time* was released in April 2020, one month into the COVID-19 pandemic and about two years after Mia finished treatment.

The heroes in *HumanKind*, like the heroes from Brad's own village, are everyday people who do what they can to make a difference. Their acts of kindness change lives. "They don't just hope the world will get better," Brad says. "They make it better."

When Brad started collecting and sharing the stories, he had no idea that the stories would become the focus of a national best seller. He just knew that he enjoyed sharing inspiring stories, that he was good at finding them and that people were uplifted by reading them—in alignment with his purpose to help people have better lives.

Today, Mia is healthy and the book has sold nearly a hundred thousand copies, with all proceeds going to Hopeworks and Big Brothers Big Sisters. Forbes describes it as "the most uplifting and life-affirming book in years." The Independent

Book Publishers Association chose it as the best inspirational book of the year, and it was an International Book Awards winner. The book has also shined a spotlight on dozens of organizations and helped them to raise money and attract new volunteers. One ripple of kindness is leading to another and another as each volunteer and every dollar feed the wheel of good—the cycle of one good act leading to another.

We know that abuse begets abuse, violence begets violence, and war begets war, but it's also true that good begets good, and we tend to underestimate the power of that positive cycle. Imagine a giant wheel that's rolling along filled with all good things, and every time we do something helpful, the wheel gets bigger. When we feed this wheel of good, the results of the ripples we make will be exponential.

Brad's goal isn't just to live a meaningful life—it's to help other people do what's important to them and actualize their potential. "I don't think this kind of commitment is a requirement and I don't think less of people who make other choices," he says, "but if I want the world to be a better place, I need to do something about it. Even if I can't change the whole world, I can change the part I'm in."

No matter how we choose to help the people in our village or in the world at large, every kind act creates a ripple effect, like a pebble that's thrown into a pond. And every other act creates a ripple too. So it's important that we recognize the impact we're having and take steps to leave the legacy we want to leave. Irvin Yalom says, "Rippling refers to the fact that each of us creates—often without our conscious intent or knowledge—concentric circles of influence that may affect others for years, even for generations. That is, the effect we have on other people is in turn passed on to others, much as the ripples in a pond go on and on until they're no longer visible but continuing at a nano level. The idea that we can leave something of ourselves, even beyond our knowing, offers a potent answer to those who claim that meaninglessness inevitably flows from one's finiteness and transiency."

We don't know how far the effects of our actions will reach or how they might help others, but we know that what we put into motion can continue long after we're gone. By strengthening our relationships and being intentional about the things we do, we can produce positive effects for people near and far. By joining together with our village, we can all help each other to be better and do better.

In a world as connected as ours, we can see that in many ways we're all part of one big village. The more we each contribute to the wheel of good, the better off we'll all be, both individually and collectively. It doesn't have to be a grand gesture—we can all make a positive impact by doing what we can where we are. Not in order to be remembered or to feed our egos but to feed the wheel of good. Together we *can* change the world.

———

IN BRIEF

- Pursuing what you're passionate about often requires courage, and so does living according to your individual values—especially when they don't align with society's definition of success or our family's.
- Living a purposeful life usually isn't the easiest path, but scientific studies and life experience show that it's the healthiest, most fulfilling path.

- A strong, connected village will help you overcome obstacles, encourage you when the learning curve is steep and support the changes you're making. Change can be scary, but when your village has your back, it's a little easier to take a chance.
- If you allow fear to stop you, whether it's fear of failure, rejection, judgment or anything else, you forfeit the freedom to leave the legacy we want to leave. The next time you think, *What if I fail?*, challenge yourself with the question "What if I fly?"
- When you're clear about the difference you want to make and you're making changes to achieve that vision, suffering and hardships are more tolerable because you know your "why."
- If you're leading a team, it's helpful when your vision and values are aligned with those of your teammates. Good leaders sell their vision and get everyone on board because they know they can achieve so much more when everyone has a shared purpose and is working toward the same goal.
- No matter how you choose to help the people in your village or in the world at large, every kind act creates a ripple effect, like a pebble that's thrown into a pond. And every other act creates a ripple too.
- By being intentional about your actions, the ripples you make can produce positive effects for people near and far, and you can expand the effects you're having by strengthening your relationships and expanding your village. With this approach, we can all be better, do better, and make a lasting impact.

RECONNECT, REMODEL, AND REPAIR

Repairing and renovating relationships can be challenging, but it's usually easier than living with the pain and damage that dysfunctional relationships cause. All it takes is one harmful relationship to undermine your overall quality of life and limit your ability to achieve your goals. So it's imperative to evaluate what you have, work on what you can fix and put boundaries in place to minimize the pain that other people can inflict on you.

Doing routine relationship "checkups" is as important for your health, happiness, and success as having routine physical exams. When you do a relationship checkup, your goal is to look for things that are realistically within your power to improve, remodel or repair.

The Action Guide offers recommendations for how to repair broken connections and remodel your relationships with parents, siblings, partners, children, friends, and the people you work with.

YOU AND YOUR PAST

Your most important relationships are the ones you have with yourself and your past. If you're not on good terms with yourself, it's much harder to repair relationships with others. There are many reasons for not having good relationships with ourselves, but the root causes are usually negative core beliefs formed during childhood and unresolved issues from our past. So that's where we'll begin:

To repair your relationship with yourself and your past:
examine the negative core beliefs you have about yourself
and formulate a plan to elevate your self-esteem.

If you believe you're not good enough or worthless, it will be impossible for you to take in the compliments and love that other people give you. If you don't believe you're worthy of respect and love, you may even think less of the people who like you the most. If this is happening in your life, you already know that your low self-esteem and negative core beliefs about yourself are huge impediments to happiness and success

Elevating your self-esteem is an essential step in repairing your relationship with yourself, and I won't say it's easy, but as grandiose as this goal may sound, you *can* achieve it, one step at a time.

HOW TO ELEVATE SELF-ESTEEM

Practice Radical Self-Acceptance

Exercising your self-acceptance "muscles" can be hard work at first, especially if you didn't feel accepted as a child or haven't used these muscles very much. Radical self-acceptance doesn't mean excusing negative behavior or harmful habits. It's not a way of letting yourself off the hook. It's a way of aligning with the reality that great people sometimes do things they're not proud of because they're human, and that includes you.

One way to enhance self-esteem and self-acceptance is to upgrade old mental programs with information that's more accurate and empowering. In other words, replace the negative self-talk with statements that focus on your strengths and aspirations. To do this intentionally and consistently, write a few true and affirming statements and commit to saying them out loud, in front of a mirror, every day. Every time you say them, include an example to remind your brain that what you're saying is true. You can use the same example each time or different ones.

Affirming Statement:
I am a good and caring person.

Specific Example:
Last week I helped my neighbor clean up her yard.

Affirming Statement:
I can be more successful.

Specific Example:
I have a good job and I'm a reliable employee.

Backing up the affirmation with a specific example allows you to reengage with those positive aspects of yourself so you can feel yourself being or doing what you're affirming. That momentary internal shift challenges and counteracts negative self-talk, and that's how the magic happens.

Now, it's your turn:

> ### Affirming Statement:
> I am worthy of love and respect.
>
> ### Specific Example:
> Write a sentence that reminds you of a specific time or times when you treated others with love and respect.

I know this practice probably seems so small that it can't possibly do any good. In fact, I've lost count of the number of clients I've had to beg to humor me and try it. But just about all of them were amazed by the difference it made.

It takes a few weeks, but once you remind yourself enough times that you're a good and worthy person and back the affirmations up with examples, you'll retrain your brain to see and experience the truth of what you're affirming. And when that happens, you just might be as amazed as my clients have been.

Affirm Your Positive Qualities

- Use the previous examples to write three affirmations and a specific example to back up each one.
- Stand in front of a mirror and set a timer for one minute.

- Look into your eyes, imagine you're observing the experience you're recalling and engage with that recollection.
- Say your affirmations out loud until the timer goes off.

Tips:

- Do this twice a day. It can help to do it just before or after something else you do twice a day like brushing your teeth or walking your dog.
- Write statements you believe and back them up with specific memories that allow you to feel the truth of what you're affirming. After thirty days, share your experience with me on LinkedIn (linkedin.com/in/patriciabathory). This works!

Identify Unresolved Issues and Focus on What You Can Control

If you're embarrassed or ashamed about your past, not being as successful as you want to be, your appearance, trauma, abuse or anything else, you're anchored to your past and that makes it virtually impossible to move forward. When you develop or try to maintain a relationship, it can feel exhausting or incredibly stressful because you're pulling that heavy weight with you. As with elevating self-esteem, making peace with yourself and your past is an ongoing process. It's worth investing in because your relationship with yourself is the only one that's guaranteed to last your entire life. Don't you want to invest in becoming the person you aspire to be?

Begin by looking at the events that cause you pain or shame from as many different perspectives as you can. Instead of revisiting these memories as the person being victimized, look at them with curiosity and see what you can discover that's useful or empowering. No one deserves to be beaten up by alcoholic parents. Nobody deserves to be raped. Nobody deserves to be shamed, bullied, humiliated or discriminated against, so the process of mourning for the life you deserved but didn't get is legitimate and necessary. Life isn't fair a lot of the time, and real healing doesn't come from wearing rose-colored glasses, so I'm not suggesting you sweep those things under the rug or dismiss how horrific they were. I'm recommending that you process these events to start your healing. It will take time, but you can stop yourself from wishing that things had been different and turn your focus toward the future, which you have the power to influence. If you're dragging a bunch of anchors behind you, though, it'll be slow going, so find ways to turn them into propellers. If your father said you'd never amount to much, instead of letting the anger or pain consume you, use it as motivation to prove him wrong and affirm your belief in yourself. Seeing how negative events in the past influenced who you are today allows you to take steps to ensure that they don't determine who you'll be tomorrow.

The Greek Stoic philosopher Epictetus said, "It is our attitude toward events, not events themselves, which we can control. Nothing is by its own nature calamitous—even death is terrible only if we fear it." This idea is liberating because there are a whole lot of things we can't control. We don't choose our parents or our past, for example, and we don't choose some of the most life-changing events and circumstances we experience, including accidents, illnesses and the loss of loved ones. What we *can* control are our thoughts, reactions, and responses.

Unlearning the habit of fretting about things you can't control and replacing it with the habit of choosing how you react will enhance the harmony in your life and produce outcomes that are more in line with the person you want to become. As with all changes you make, this one will take practice, but it doesn't have to take a lot of time. Many of my clients find it helpful to recite the Serenity Prayer in addition to saying their affirmations. Some of them replace the word *God* with *Great Spirit, Universe, Self*, their own name or something else that resonates as true to them:

God, grant me the serenity to accept the things I cannot change, courage to change the things I can, and wisdom to know the difference.[1]

This little prayer is packed with psychological wisdom. When your goal is to focus on what you can control, it doesn't make sense to waste time or energy ruminating or wishing things were different. Instead, devote your resources to choosing a response that can make a positive difference. And when you can't change something, invest your resources in something you *can* improve.

REPAIRING CONNECTIONS WITH OTHERS

The fastest way to improve any relationship is to replace your expectations with curiosity. Instead of holding people to your standards, learn more about who they are and what's important to them. By doing this, you can deepen and expand your understanding and broaden your thinking. You may discover that the person you thought was rude is actually a very kind and generous introvert. The key is to appreciate the riches that each person wants to offer. When you do that, you'll quickly find out that everyone has valuable talents and traits.

The practice of sharing expectations, adjusting them and compromising that we covered in Chapter Six is crucial when you're repairing a relationship, so start noticing when an unmet expectation triggers you emotionally and work on adjusting it.

One of the most unrealistic assumptions is that one relationship can fulfill all your needs. People can make this mistake with friends, partners, siblings, parents, and even their kids. Instead of falling into this trap, notice how each of your relationships satisfies different needs and desires. That's why you want to build a village instead of developing just one or two close connections. One person can't be your "everything," so instead of holding on to that fantasy, why not be curious and open about what each person offers? Then you can appreciate whatever they bring to the relationship. Without the weight of expectations, relationships can rise to their highest potential.

If you're feeling resentful toward someone, there's a good chance they didn't live up to one of your expectations. The bigger the gap is between how we think someone should behave and how they do behave, the more unhappy we'll be. The ironic twist of human nature is that we're initially interested in or fascinated by someone's differences, but over time we lose that appreciation and try to get them to be more like us. So instead of benefiting from the color and spice of divergent opinions and behaviors, we try to annihilate what we initially found attractive.

To improve connections, be aware of and resist the very human inclinations to:

- Want one person to fulfill all your needs and desires
- Lose appreciation for what's different or divergent

When we align expectations with what's possible, relationships naturally improve.

PARENTS

Our parents have the most important influence on our lives as children and, consequently, in who we become as adults. No matter what we think of them, we have an innate need for their love and approval that's hard to transcend, so their actions and words tend to have a disproportionate impact on us compared with things that other people say or do. That's why we can still "hear" our parents' words many years after they were said. If they were kind and approving, your self-talk probably reflects that. And if they were cruel and disapproving, your self-talk is likely to mirror *that*, at least until you do the work to replace their voice with your own.

When we're kids, most of us see our parents as superheroes. They can do no wrong and we believe whatever they say. They can solve any problem, fix anything and heal our wounds. But around adolescence, most kids become more autonomous and start to notice that their picture-perfect parents aren't so perfect. At that age, they differentiate from their parents and want to be seen and respected as individuals. And when parents don't respect their adolescents' individuality and opinions, it encourages them to rebel and become resentful.

As we enter adulthood, it's not uncommon for that resentment to grow as our judgments become even harsher:

- They were too hard on us or not hard enough.
- They were too coddling or too cold.

It's an endless list that tends to highlight what we had too much of and what was missing. Since what we focus on tends to grow, if we dwell on this list we can unconsciously make the relationship with our parents worse.

How to Strengthen the Connection with Your Parents

Parents aren't replaceable, and ending the relationship with them comes at such a high emotional cost that it's usually worth trying to improve these relationships.

Stop Wishing for the Parents You Didn't and Don't Have
Being as objective as you can be, consider what kind of relationship is possible with each of your parents based on exactly who they are. The perfect parents (who I'm pretty sure only exist in fiction and fantasies) are a secure port to which you can always return. They're stable, provide a sensible sounding board, respect your individuality and forgive your long absences. In reality, even parents who model these ideals sometimes fall short. At the other end of the spectrum are parents who harmed their children and need to be kept at a safe distance to prevent further damage in adulthood. But most parents are somewhere between those extremes. Considering where your parents are on this spectrum can help you to determine what's realistically possible for your relationship.

By accepting your parents as they are and replacing resistance with curiosity, you may discover aspects of them you've never seen. Keep in mind that because you have an innate need for your parents' approval, love and appreciation, their opinions and actions can have a disproportionate influence on your life, and this influence can be multiplied by your own unrealistic expectations. Are you investing time and effort trying to accomplish the impossible or the very unlikely, such as pleasing consistently critical parents? Are you looking for love, approval, or attention even though they haven't filled those needs in the past?

Aim for the Best Relationship That's Possible
Being familiar with who your parents actually are is liberating. It frees you to focus on developing the best relationship that's realistically achievable. Instead of trying to change them, you have the opportunity to change the way you interact with them, keeping their limitations—and your own—in mind.

You may have parents who are super-critical and think everything you do is wrong or not good enough. Your parents may be hard-core complainers who are never happy about anything. Or they might be out of touch, disengaged, not very helpful or egocentric. While I wish I could offer a fix for all the issues you may be confronting, the way your parents trigger you is specific to your situation. So here's what I suggest:

- Try to identify specific reasons that the relationship isn't going well. In your opinion, why are your parents so annoying and difficult?
- Try to identify how the personality trait you don't like hurts you, and then identify where you see them display this trait with other people. For example, if you're hurt by your parents' criticism and you observe that they criticize other people, it's easier to take it less personally. They're not just critical of you—it's how they act with other people too.
- Once you figure this out, you can shift your thinking from:

- "My parents are super-critical of *me*" to "My parents are super-critical people."
- "My parents are always complaining and never happy with anything *I* do" to "My parents are complainers—they're never happy with *anything*."
- "My parents are very absent from my life—they don't love me" to "My parents are disengaged in general."

Ultimately, you shift from "It's about you" to "It's about them." This helps you to see that your parents' personality trait has nothing to do with you even though it affects you. It's not personal.

Another way to invest in the best relationship that's possible is to connect with your siblings to compare stories and vent. Your siblings may offer solutions or techniques they use that you haven't considered. If nothing else, reminiscing and comparing notes about your parents' idiosyncrasies can be comic relief. Humor can be a relationship power tool. You might even let your parents in on the joke. Sometimes, making light of grouchiness, complaining or criticizing can help improve these relationships, one joke at a time.

Whether you use humor or other tools, the ultimate quest is to learn to be less affected by your parents' negative personality traits.

Reignite Your Admiration for Them If Possible, and Extend Forgiveness If Not

As you become older and your responsibilities increase in size and number, it's easy to lose appreciation for the ways your parents did things. That may not seem like a big deal, but when appreciation goes, it takes admiration and respect with it and the relationship suffers.

To reignite admiration or move toward forgiveness, I ask my clients to tell me the stories that explain why they're upset with their parents, but from their parents' perspectives instead of their own. As the stories unfold from the parents' viewpoints and they walk in their shoes, they see their parents' faults and shortcomings in a new frame of reference. This type of reframing fosters compassion and minimizes judgment. If you realize that your parents did the best they could with what they had to work with and that, given the same circumstances, you probably wouldn't have been able to do it much differently, your disappointment and resentment can be replaced with empathy and understanding. That's better for them and much better for you. I'm so grateful when my clients experience this night-and-day difference. Frowns literally turn upside down. That momentous turning point gives them a better view of their parents' attributes.

It's also worth mentioning that while research in child psychology was being conducted in the 20th century, much of that information didn't reach the public until about fifty years ago. So it's not fair to compare our parents' child-rearing approach with our own because we have access to thousands of books and other resources that highlight the importance of valuing children's feelings and preferences. We also have abundant research about the effects of different parenting dynamics, so while there's no formula for raising kids, today's parents can be much more knowledgeable and better-equipped than our parents were. Imagine how much harder parenting would be if you didn't know all the things your parents didn't know. That can lead to greater empathy at the very least.

If reigniting outright admiration isn't possible—and unfortunately there are many cases when it's not—then the best relationship to strive for may be one that's as harmonious as possible. No matter what your parents do, you can choose to let go of some of your resentment and maybe work on forgiveness so that the way forward is paved with peaceful interactions. And when that isn't a viable option, the only healthy choice might be to disengage. If that's the situation you're in, remember that even though some scars last forever, you were strong enough to survive and you're strong enough to heal and thrive.

BROTHERS AND SISTERS

During the first years of our lives, we live comfortably or uncomfortably close with other children who we're expected to love and get along with. They share our parents and our history, and they're the only ones besides our parents who witness our childhood. This can be a setup for a close and loyal bond, an antagonistic disconnection or anything in between. But unless the damage is irreparable, research studies affirm that having an amicable relationship with siblings is worth striving for. Even though there are instances where cutting ties with them is tempting, it might take a bigger toll on your psychological energy than keeping a civil, see-you-once-a-year kind of relationship with them.

Dr. Shawn Sidhu, a psychiatrist at University of New Mexico Health Sciences, found that the relationships with our siblings are often the longest relationships of our lives,[2] so it's worth considering how we can develop or at least maintain them. Research also shows that in our later years, the connections we have with our siblings may be the most valuable for our physical and mental health. For example, a Swedish study found that having satisfying relationships with our siblings when we're in our eighties is more closely correlated with health and positive mood than good relationships with friends or adult children.[3] And having a close connection with siblings can make a dramatic difference because support from people who have known you the longest increases the likelihood that you'll realize your ambitions, achieve your dreams, and leave a legacy.

But getting to a good place with siblings can be a complex endeavor. You might have incompatible personalities, different values, or baggage from the past. Sometimes you just get busy and drift apart. Other times, siblings are estranged and don't even know why.

How to Repair Connections with Siblings

Evaluate the Cost of the Rivalry or Estrangement

Is it draining energy that you could be using to accomplish your goals? How invested are you in keeping this separation in place? How might you benefit by restoring the relationship to an amicable level? What might happen if you go "all in" and invest in the relationship to reap all its potential benefits?

Stop Wishing for Siblings You Don't Have and Find Authentic Reasons to be More Grateful for the Ones You Do Have

If you only see shortcomings in your siblings, by looking at them with more generosity, compassion, and curiosity you can find qualities you appreciate and admire. Plus, your siblings are the only people you share decades of inside family jokes with.

PARTNER OR SPOUSE

Unlike your family of origin, you *choose* your partner. But then, with time, your partner becomes your family and, as such, less of a choice. When you're going through rough patches, you can't take time off or distance yourself a little like you can with parents, siblings, and friends. You're invested in the relationship and want to find a way to make life more harmonious, but you may have different ideas about how money should be spent, saved and invested, different opinions about what marriage means and what makes a good one, and if you're raising a family, you probably have differences about rules, rewards, and punishments. On the most basic, day-to-day level, the differences can be minimal but grating. You want the toilet seat to be kept down and the lid closed and your partner thinks it's a ridiculous thing to care so much about. They think the lawn should be manicured and you think drought-resistant wildflowers are the way to go. Over time, small differences can add up, and instead of focusing on what you have in common and like about each other, you start to fixate on your differences and what you don't appreciate.

How to Repair Your Connection with Your Partner

Examine Your Complaints
Begin by making a list of your top three to five complaints. Next, consider whether each complaint is being caused by something they can change or if it's the result of a personality trait. Wanting an introverted spouse to become the life of the party is unrealistic, but wanting them to cordially greet your friends and houseguests is reasonable.

If you want your partner to be more romantic, surprise you with thoughtful gifts or favors or go out dancing with you and they don't accommodate you, it doesn't mean they don't care about you or don't love you. People have different ways of expressing their love and affection and certain ways they want to be loved, but don't let those preferences overshadow the reality of how your partner *is* loving you. Do they keep your gas tank topped off? Do they make dinner? Pack lunches for the kids? Do your laundry? Schedule your car maintenance? Pay attention to the meaning you're assigning to what your partner does and doesn't do. And examine that meaning to see if you're arriving at conclusions that just aren't true. Everything is imbued with the meaning you give it.

Instead of sticking with a negative narrative, you can choose to assign a good meaning to your partner's actions. For example, if your partner is working long hours, you can focus on the sacrifice they're making for your future together instead of complaining about how little attention they're giving you right now. If you want to be happier with your partner, create a narrative that's fit for the queen or king you want them to be. There's no good reason to stay stuck in a negative rut when you can liberate yourself simply by expanding your lens and shifting your point of view. Sometimes, a simple reframing of your current situation can initiate a series of positive changes.

Reconnect With Your Initial Attraction

Take a trip down memory lane and revisit why you were attracted to your partner when you first met. What qualities made them special? How did you feel when you were with them and why? What did you tell your friends about how the two of you complemented each other?

What you'll probably discover is that some of the things you're annoyed by are the things you found attractive at the beginning of your relationship.

Initially Attractive
He lets me pick any restaurant or movie I want.

Now Annoying
He never takes the initiative to make plans.
I have to make all the decisions myself.

Initially Attractive
He's so on top of everything! He organized the pantry,
made a spreadsheet for the bills and even made a
maintenance schedule for the appliances.

Now Annoying
He's so controlling! He tries to micromanage everything I do. Last
week he gave me a list of what I should clean every week and what
cleaning product I'm supposed to use. Are you freaking kidding me?

Initially Attractive
She spends hours getting ready for our dates and
always looks like a million bucks from head to toe.

Now Annoying
It takes forever for her to get ready to go out, even if we're just going
for pizza. Does she have to look like a Christmas tree every time?

Initially Attractive
Finally, I have a girlfriend who has a life of her own. She never
complains about me working late or going out with my friends.

Now Annoying
She's so self-absorbed. All she cares about is herself. If I
disappeared tomorrow, I don't think she'd notice.

Remembering how you found these characteristics appealing in the beginning can help you refresh and reframe their meaning.

CHILDREN

Every parent dreams about what their children will be like, what they'll do together as they grow up and sometimes even what they hope their children will "become." That's understandable. But if you believe your kids are going to want to create your idea of their dream life, you're kidding yourself. A natural part of growing up is for children to start differentiating themselves from their parents and their parents' dreams. They want to be heard, respected and treated as individuals, and this is when the conflict tends to begin. But if you know that your kids are meant to grow up to be unique individuals, not replicas of you, it will be rewarding for you to encourage their dreams and celebrate their choices. If you can't yet find it in yourself to do this, at least don't say or do anything that could seriously damage your relationship with them.

Having a strained relationship with your children can cause a lot of emotional pain, and many parents consider it a personal failure even when they've tried everything to make the relationship better. When children cut ties with their parents, it can cause profound uncertainty and grief. The parents often feel abandoned and worry that the child believes *they're* the ones who abandoned *them*. There are no winners in this scenario.

A survey of more than eight hundred people conducted by Lucy Blake, author of *No Family is Perfect: A Guide to Embracing the Messy Reality*, shows that when parents and adult children are estranged, it's usually the child who broke the connection.[4] The reasons adult children disconnect from parents fall on the spectrum from clashes in values to having been emotionally, physically, or sexually abused. Along that spectrum are also adults who felt overwhelmed by their parents when they were children and pushed back as they became older and more independent. Another reason adult children pull back is that they feel too much responsibility for their parents' happiness. I often hear estranged children request better boundaries from their parents as a condition of reconciliation. As Andrew Solomon wrote in *Far From the Tree: Parents, Children and the Search for Identity*, "There is no contradiction between loving someone and feeling burdened by that person. Indeed, love tends to magnify the burden."

Regardless of the reason for the rift, parents often blame the estrangement on their divorce, the child's partner or the child's sense of entitlement. It's hard for parents to accept that their adult children might feel a sense of relief or freedom in ending the relationship; parents usually report feeling deep shame, loss, grief, personal failure and regret.

How to Repair Your Relationship with Your Children

Respect Your Child's Individuality and Choices
Many parents see their children as extensions of themselves rather than recognizing that their children are unique individuals. Instead of making assumptions about them, our job is to learn about them.

If you've gotten into the habit of speaking for your children, it's not too late to retrain yourself. For example, instead of saying, "No, she won't like that," say something like "I don't think she'll like that, but let's ask or we'll never know." Kids change their likes and dislikes as they navigate the challenging task of becoming adults. Sometimes they don't even know what they like or don't like, so how can we be so sure?

It's a tenuous line parents have to walk between guiding them and giving them space to figure out what their preferences are and what's important to them. When they become teenagers, we have to give them some autonomy over their lives and accept their need to differentiate themselves from us. Being an authoritative "my way or the highway" parent may make kids obedient short-term, but it doesn't foster respect. To build a loving, trusting and respectful relationship with teens, we need to listen to them and learn about them. We still get the last word on curfew time and those types of rules until they're eighteen, but respectfully listening to them with an open mind when they explain why they want to bend or change a particular rule goes a long way—even when we don't agree. What they'll remember is how we took the time to hear their rationale. When they become adults, this is even more important, so you might as well start practicing when they're adolescents. If this hasn't been one of your strengths, it's not too late to get better at this. You won't get immediate results, but if you're consistent, you're bound to see improvement.

Don't Act Like They Owe You Something

Don't expect gratitude from your children or, worse, tell them they *should* be grateful for all you've done and sacrificed for them. They didn't ask you to have them or adopt them. No matter what the circumstances of their conception and birth are, they don't share any of the responsibility for the outcome. So it's not fair to expect gratitude. It's nice to have it—don't get me wrong. As Cicero said, "Gratitude is not only the greatest of virtues, but the parent of all others." But it shouldn't be expected as "payback" for raising your kids. The payback was the love, affection, and giggles you got. Gratitude is extra, the cherry on top.

Sometimes kids won't realize how grateful they are until they grow up and have their own children. My friend Tom didn't think much about the sacrifices his father made for him until he was making similar sacrifices for his own sons, including driving them to hockey practice, games and even tournaments in distant cities. "I realized that my dad did all of this for me without ever complaining or saying a word about it," he told me.

His father was still alive, so Tom got to tell him how grateful he was, which was wonderful for both of them. But sometimes the insight that allows your children to be grateful comes long after you're gone. And hopefully this will be okay with you, because the minute you attach expectation to your relationship, you threaten your connection with them.

I'm including the first few sentences of one my favorite writings about children because the parents I know who follow this guidance tend to have much more fulfilling relationships with their children.

On Children

Your children are not your children.
They are the sons and daughters of Life's longing for itself.
They come through you but not from you,
And though they are with you yet they belong not to you.
– Kahlil Gibran[5]

FRIENDS

There's a lot of truth to the expression that friends are the family we choose. Since the choosing is mutual, friendships can be fabulous relationships. You like each other, so it's easy to get along, you may have more in common with friends than you have with your partner or your children, and friends don't have to navigate the challenges inherent in partnerships and marriages. And when a friendship is new, it's a fresh start that doesn't come with emotional baggage like relationships with parents and siblings do.

Sometimes, though, we're not as intentional with our actions and words and over time that can weaken our connection. Jokes that are hurtful; canceling plans at the last minute; and not being careful with your communication because they "get you," are examples of the ways we can unintentionally weaken a relationship.

How to Repair Your Connection with Your Friends

Be Open and Honest
When a friendship feels strained, it's often because of miscommunication, distancing due to life's demands, or growing apart, so the first step is to tell your friend what you're experiencing and ask if they've been feeling something similar. Whether or not they have, you can analyze what's at the root of your feelings and find a path forward together.

Make Your Friend a Priority
Once you identify the problem and decide on a repair plan, don't drop the ball because you're too busy. Typically, people are too busy only when it comes to doing things they don't

want to do. Prioritizing the friendship means investing in it just like you invest in other things you value, so be purposeful in your friendship. Schedule calls and visits, organize events, be a supportive member of your friend's village and celebrate their accomplishments.

Keep Confiding in Them

Confiding in your friend is a form of emotional intimacy that protects your connection against erosion. So don't let this part of your friendship fall by the wayside when you're feeling overwhelmed by life's daily demands. You need to connect with your friends frequently and allow enough time to dive beneath the superficial to the more meaningful exchanges that sustain and fortify friendships.

PEOPLE AT WORK
(BOSS, CO-WORKERS, EMPLOYEES)

Before retirement, adults spend about half their waking hours at work, so if you're not getting along with your boss, co-workers or employees, conflict and turmoil will consume nearly a third of your life and undermine your health.

Research conducted by Leigh Branham, author of *The 7 Hidden Reasons Employees Leave*, shows that only 12 percent of employees leave an organization because they want to make more money.[6] The vast majority leave because they're unhappy with the work they do or the people they work with or for. According to The Conference Board, a nonprofit research organization, 53 percent of Americans are unhappy at work.

Another study that was conducted over ten years with two hundred thousand participants found that 79 percent of people who quit their jobs said it was mainly because they weren't appreciated.[7] The study found that when employees feel recognized by their managers, they give them higher ratings for communication, goal-setting, trust, and accountability.

If you're a leader, you can improve employee satisfaction and retention by improving your relationship with your employees and creating a harmonious, cooperative culture. If you're an employee, you may be waiting for your boss or someone higher up in management to improve the culture, but 58 percent of the managers in a CareerBuilder.com study said they hadn't received any management training, so your leadership team may not know how to do this or even know that people are leaving because of the current culture. You can help to lead the change by encouraging management to foster gratitude and better relationships by introducing initiatives and suggesting workshops that help people to learn and use relationship best practices.

How to Repair Relationships at Work

One of the most efficient ways to repair work relationships is to focus on improving the work environment and company culture.

See Yourself as Part of the Team

Whether you're a manager, employee or owner of the business, you're all in the same village, working toward the same goals. Being a valuable member of the team requires trust and open communication, two of the core ingredients that strengthen relationships and forge strong bonds. By treating everyone equally, you can start to shift the mentality from competitive to cooperative no matter what your role in the organization is.

If you're the boss or the owner, fostering a collaborative environment will create more meaningful relationships for you and your employees and radically reduce turnover costs.

Show Appreciation for Everyone You Work With

The most powerful change you can make is to develop the habit of showing your appreciation. If this doesn't come naturally to you, set a daily goal for how many people you'll thank and track and record your progress. Everyone needs community, meaningful connections and validation. When you assign yourself the role of gratitude cultivator, you can help everyone to feel more appreciated, including yourself.

Karl Sun, co-founder and CEO of Lucidchart and Lucid Software, says, "Gratitude is a basic human requirement—and since we spend most of our waking hours at the office, giving and receiving thanks at work becomes pretty important."[8] There's evidence that the benefits of gratitude in the workplace are even more important than self-worth and self-efficacy, possibly because gratitude can be contagious. By expressing your appreciation for what someone says or does, you can create a ripple effect that uplifts your whole department.

Gratitude improves physical and mental health, enhances self-esteem and mental resilience, aids sleep, amplifies empathy and curbs aggression. So the better you get at fostering gratitude in the workplace, the better off everyone will be.

Maintain a Positive Attitude

Being criticized, falling short of expectations, not meeting goals, having your contribution overlooked, being ignored or disregarded in a meeting and being asked to take on more responsibility without being paid more are just a few of the situations that can test our emotional maturity. The challenge is to rise above the urge to be negative, vindictive, defensive, petty or disgruntled when these things happen.

Maintaining a positive attitude means:

- Acknowledging that you're responsible for creating a pleasant workplace so that you and the people you work with can all do your best.
- Responding to criticism and feedback by being open to things you can improve instead of feeling personally attacked.
- Treating everyone with respect, no matter how they're behaving.
- Learning to see challenges and problems as opportunities.

ENDNOTES

CHAPTER 1

1. Fang, Yiwei, Bill Francis, Iftekhar Hansan. 2018. "Differences make a difference: Diversity in social learning and value creation." *Journal of Corporate Finance*, 48 (February):474-491. https://doi.org/10.1016/j.jcorpfin.2017.11.015.

2. Fang, Yiwei, Bill Francis, Iftekhar Hasan. 2018. "Research: CEOs with Diverse Networks Create Higher Firm Value." *Harvard Business Review*, April 10, 2018. https://hbr.org/2018/04/research-ceos-with-diverse-networks-create-higher-firm-value.

3. Wolff, Hans-Georg, Klaus Moser. 2009. "Effects of networking on career success: a longitudinal study." *Journal of Applied Psychology* 94 (1): 196-206. https://pubmed.ncbi.nlm.nih.gov/19186904/.

4. Simpson, Jeffry A. 1990. "Influence of attachment styles on romantic relationships." *Journal of Personality and Social Psychology* 59 (5): 971-980. https://doi.org/10.1037/0022-3514.59.5.971.

CHAPTER 2

1. Smith, Emily E. 2017. *The Power of Meaning: Crafting a Life that Matters*. New York: Crown.

2. Frankl, Viktor E. 2006. *Man's Search for Meaning*. Boston: Beacon Press.

3. Baumeister, Roy F., Kathleen D. Vohs, Jennifer L. Aaker, Emily N. Garbinsky. 2013. "Some key differences between a happy life and a meaningful life." *The Journal of Positive Psychology* 8 (6): 505-516. https://www.tandfonline.com/doi/abs/10.1080/17439760.2013.830764.

4. Fredrickson, Barbara L., Karen M. Grewen, Kimberly A. Coffey, Sara B. Algoe, Ann M. Firestine, Jesusa M. G. Arevalo, Jeffrey Ma, Steven W. Cole. 2013. "A functional genomic perspective on human well-being." *Proceedings of the National Academy of Sciences* 110 no. 33 (August): 13684-13689. https://pubmed.ncbi.nlm.nih.gov/23898182/.

5. Klein, Howard J., Robert B. Lount Jr., Hee Man Park, Bryce J. Linford. 2020. "When goals are known: The effects of audience relative status on goal commitment and performance." *Journal of Applied Psychology* 105 (4): 372-389. https://psycnet.apa.org/doi/10.1037/apl0000441.

CHAPTER 3

1. Pearson, Catherine. 2022. "How Many Friends Do You Really Need?" *The New York Times*, May 7, 2022. https://www.nytimes.com/2022/05/07/well/live/adult-friendships-number.html.

2. Degges-White, Suzanne, Marcela Kepic. 2020. "Friendships, Subjective Age, and Life Satisfaction of Women in Midlife." *Adultspan Journal* 19 (1): 39-53. https://onlinelibrary.wiley.com/doi/10.1002/adsp.12086.

CHAPTER 4

1. Miller, William R., Janet C'de Baca, Daniel B. Matthews, Paula L. Wilbourne. "Personal Values Card Sort." 2001, University of New Mexico Department of Psychology. https://casaa.unm.edu/inst/personal%20values%20card%20sort.pdf.

2. Yalom, Irvin D. 1980. *Existential Psychotherapy*. United States: BasicBooks.

CHAPTER 5

1. Mehrabian, Albert. 1971. *Silent Messages*. Belmont: Wadsworth Publishing.

2. Hester, Neil. 2019. "Perceived Negative Emotion in Neutral Faces: Gender-Dependent Effects on Attractiveness and Threat." *American Psychological Association* 19 (8): 1490-1494. https://psycnet.apa.org/doiLanding?doi=10.1037%2Femo0000525.

CHAPTER 6

1. Thurman, Dan. 2023. "Relative Reality." Motivations Works Inc. https://danthurmon.com/relative-reality/.

2. Mark, Joshua J. 2009. "Protagoras." *World History Encyclopedia*. Last modified September 2, 2009. https://www.worldhistory.org/protagoras/.

3. Hartung, Freda-Marie, Pia Thieme, Nele Wild-Wall, Benedikt Hell. 2022. "Being snoopy and smart: The relationship between curiosity, fluid intelligence, and knowledge." *Journal of Individual Differences* 43 (4): 194–205. https://doi.org/10.1027/1614-0001/a000372.

4. Gino, Francesca. 2018. "The Business Case for Curiosity." *Harvard Business Review*, September-October 2018. https://hbr .org/2018/09/the-business-case-for-curiosity.

5. Porter, Tenelle, Karina Schumann. 2018. "Intellectual humility and openness to the opposing view." *Self and Identity* 17 (2): 139-162. https://doi.org/10.1080/15298868.2017.1361 861.

CHAPTER 7

1. Jensen, Susan M., Fred Luthans. 2006. "Entrepreneurs as authentic leaders: Impact on employees' attitudes." *Leadership & Organization Development Journal* 27 (8): 646-666. https:// psycnet.apa.org/doi/10.1108/01437730610709273.

2. van den Bosch, Ralph, Toon W. Taris. 2014. "Authenticity at work: Development and validation of an individual authenticity measure at work." *Journal of Happiness Studies: An Interdisciplinary Forum on Subjective Well-Being* 15 (1): 1-18. https://psycnet.apa.org/doi/10.1007/s10902-013-9413-3.

3. Conroy, Catherine. 2018. "You could miss someone every day and still be glad they're not in your life." *The Irish Times*, February 24, 2018. https://www.irishtimes.com/life-and-style/ people/you-could-miss-someone-every-day-and-still-be-glad -they-re-not-in-your-life-1.3393409.

CHAPTER 9

1. Viktor E. Frankl, *Man's Search for Meaning* (Boston: Beacon Press, 2006).

RELATIONSHIP ACTION GUIDE

1. Wikipedia contributors, "Serenity Prayer," *Wikipedia, The Free Encyclopedia*, https://en.wikipedia.org/w/index. php?title=Serenity_Prayer&oldid=1178052804 (accessed October 19, 2023).

2. Sidhu, Shawn. 2019. "The Importance of Siblings." *Health Sciences Newsroom*, January 7, 2019. https://hsc.unm.edu/news/ news/the-importance-of-siblings.html.

3. McCamish-Svensson, Cheryl, Gillis Samuelsson, Bo Hagberg, Torbjörn Svensson, Ove Dehlin. 1999. "Social relationships and health as predictors of life satisfaction in advanced old age: Results from a Swedish longitudinal study." *The International Journal of Aging & Human Development* 48 (4): 301-324. https://psycnet.apa.org/doi/10.2190/GX0K-565H -08FB-XF5G.

4. Blake, Lucy, Becca Bland, Susan Golombok. 2015. "Hidden Voices: Family Estrangement in Adulthood." University of Cambridge Centre for Family Research. Stand Alone. December 10, 2015. https://www.standalone.org.uk/wp-content/uploads/2015/12/HiddenVoices.FinalReport.pdf.

5. Gibran, Kahlil 1923. "On Children" in *The Prophet*, 21-22. New York: Knopf (reprinted by Vail-Ballou Press).

6. Strut, David, Todd Nordstrom. 2018. "10 Shocking

Workplace Stats You Need To Know." *Forbes*, March 8, 2018.
https://www.forbes.com/sites/davidsturt/2018/03/08/10
-shocking-workplace-stats-you-need-to-
know/?sh=36be2b4f3afe.

7. "Performance Accelerated: A New Benchmark for Initiating
Employee Engagement, Retention and Results." O.C. Tanner
Learning Group. https://f.hubspotusercontent10.net/
hubfs/8011865/MLS_Group_July2020/PDF/White_Paper_
Performance_Accelerated.pdf.

8. Westover, Jonathan H. 2020. "The Benefits of
Showing Gratitude In The Workplace." *Forbes*,
December 29, 2020. https://www.forbes.com/sites/
forbescoachescouncil/2021/12/29/the-benefits-of-showing
-gratitude-in-the-workplace/?sh=493759d817dd.

ACKNOWLEDGMENTS

To my clients, the changes you make and the steps you take to live the life you aspire to are inspiring. You reinforce my belief that improving our relationship skills can make us happier, healthier, and more successful. Thank you for allowing me to feed the wheel of good by sharing your stories. The most intimate is also the most universal so your experiences will help others to navigate their journeys.

To my teachers, professors and mentors, standing on your shoulders allowed me to see how relationships affect every aspect of our lives and understand that strengthening our connections gives us the best chance for success.

To the researchers toiling until untold hours in your quest to unravel the mysteries of human relationships, I'm so grateful for your work. I salute you.

Elizabeth Wallace, thank you for taking me under your wing when I arrived in Canada and explaining what the requirements were for a psychoanalysis practice and how to get the credentials I needed. I'm so grateful for your guidance.

To my psychotherapy colleagues, thank you for generously sharing your insights about the connection between relationships and success. Shout out to Derrick Shirley for the fine work you're doing to help men navigate relationships in our rapidly changing world.

Irvin Yalom, your existential psychotherapy model, "here and now" approach and therapeutic techniques form the foundation of my private practice and are making a significant difference in my clients' lives. From the bottom of my heart, thank you.

Malcolm Gladwell, thank you for having the courage to explore a wide variety of perspectives and revisit commonly accepted "truths." The theories you present in your books and the discussions you have on your *Revisionist Theory* podcast are brilliant illustrations of exchanging certainty for curiosity.

Ronaldo Pereira, Alberio Bathory-Frota, Daniela Castro, Lara Bezerra, and Brad Aronson, thank you for the positive difference you're making in your villages and the ripple effects you're creating around the world. It's an honor to share your success stories. Brad, thank you also for generously sharing your knowledge about the business of selling books.

Windword Literary Services, thank you for supporting my vision for this book from concept development through editing. Toni Robino, your book architecture process made it easy to organize my ideas and build a beautiful book. Thank you for your incredibly high standards, having such high expectations of me and assuring me that I could exceed them. Doug Wagner, your keen insights and editing made my manuscript shine. Thank you both for helping my dream to write this book come true. My gratitude is infinite.

Josh Linkner and Kristen Ziman, thank you for sharing your insights about the publishing industry and your experience as professional speakers.

Amplify Publishing Group, thank you for believing in this book and for bringing it to life. Naren Aryal, thank you for going above and beyond! To Will Wolfslau, Jenna Scafuri, and the Amplify design team, I appreciate your expertise, professionalism and enthusiasm.

To everyone in my village, I'm so grateful for your unwavering support in my life and during this project. You cheered me on, checked in to see how I was doing and had complete faith in my ability to bring this project to fruition.

Mom, thank you for telling me I should write a book and encouraging me to do it. (Don't give up on my novel. It may be in the future after all.)

Tico, thank you for reading my chapter drafts, talking through my ideas for this book with me and helping me to decide what was most meaningful for readers. Climbing this mountain was much more fun and less scary with you by my side.

Bela and Sasa, thank you for keeping me on my toes and making sure I don't take myself too seriously. You make life infinitely better. I love you more than I thought it was possible to love.

Lauro, thank you for believing in me every step of the way and especially when I take big leaps of faith. The longer we're together, the more I love you and appreciate your certainty that "It's all going to work out." You are my parachute.

BIG BROTHERS BIG SISTERS OF AMERICA RECEIVES 100 PERCENT OF THE PROCEEDS FROM THE SALE OF THIS BOOK.

Why Big Brothers Big Sisters of America?

Because I believe that relationships are the most significant factor in whether we'll achieve success, I'm reverting the proceeds from book sales to a nonprofit that invests in human potential by facilitating positive relationships between adult mentors and children. Big Brothers Big Sisters' vision is for "All youth to achieve their full potential," and by supporting this organization we can have a positive impact on the lives of young people in our community.

For more than 120 years, Big Brothers Big Sisters has supported the inherent potential in every child by matching adult volunteers ("Bigs") and kids ("Littles") ages five through young adulthood in communities across the country. Partnering with parents and guardians, volunteers and other community members, BBBS strengthens communities by helping children to realize their potential and build their futures.

Research conducted on the impact of BBBS' mentoring found that the relationships that Big Brothers and Big Sisters have with young people create substantial benefits. Jean Baldwin Grossman and team reported: "At the conclusion of the 18-month study period, we found that Little Brothers and Little Sisters were less likely to have started using drugs or alcohol, felt more competent about doing school work, attended school more, got better grades, and had better relationships with their parents and peers than they would have had they not participated in the program."

The mentoring relationships pave the way for these kids to achieve the success they're seeking and strengthen their communities. If you're inspired by the work this organization is doing, you can feed the wheel of good and support Big Brothers Big Sisters to help others to succeed, by:

- Give *Connected: Building Relationships to Achieve Success and Make a Lasting Impact* to the people in your village
- Share the book on your social media channels
- Write a book review and share it with us on social media
- Connect with me on LinkedIn and help to promote the book: linkedin.com/in/patriciabathory

You can also support Big Brothers Big Sisters directly by making a financial donation and volunteering.

To donate, visit:
bbbs.org/donate

To get involved, visit:
bbbs.org/get-involved

We can all be better and do better by strengthening our connections and feeding the wheel of good.

ABOUT THE AUTHOR

Patricia Bathory, MBA, MACP, CCC, believes that relationships are the most significant factor in whether we'll achieve success. For the past eight years, in addition to running her trading business and seeing clients, Patricia has been researching and studying interpersonal dynamics, including how our relationships directly affect our ability to succeed in business and in life. She wholeheartedly believes that by improving our relationship skills and strengthening our connections, we feed the wheel of good and position ourselves to make a lasting impact.

As a psychotherapist and the founder and general manager of an import/export business, Patricia has a blend of experience that gives her unique insight into the personal and professional problems that entrepreneurs and leaders face every day. As a wife and mother, she's also well-acquainted with the challenges that go hand in hand with marriage and raising a family.

Patricia's experience and expertise make her a sought-after speaker for companies large and small, civic organizations, and NGOs on topics ranging from curiosity and intellectual humility to existential purpose. Her keynotes inspire audience members to learn how to get along with anybody, moderate conflicts, and navigate difficult relationship dynamics.

Patricia has master's degrees in business administration and counseling psychology and advanced training in psychoanalysis and family and group dynamics. She was born in Brazil, educated in Canada, and has family in the United States—so she lives here, there, and everywhere.